H

A Picaresque Novel in Verse

by

Matt Flumerfelt

Aakenbaaken & Kent   New York

A Picaresque Novel in Verse

Copyright 2016 by Matt Flumerfelt, all rights reserved.

No part of this book may be used or reproduced in any manner whatsoever without written permission except in the case of brief quotations for use in articles and reviews.

Aakenbaaken & Kent   New York

aakenbaakeneditor@gmail.com

Cover drawing courtesy of Jason Looper.

ISBN: 978-1-938436-21-5

Dedication

This book is affectionately dedicated to Charles "Chuck" Eastridge, a young man of heroic proportions who died far too soon, and to my wife, Cosima, a hero in her own right.

He does not scorn to work by lowly
means a high and marvelous effect.

Tasso

Prologue

Before man first began to dwell
beneath the sun's ethereal light,
all was confusion, one dismal hell,
abysmal darkness and eternal night,
when out of elemental strife
came love and primal sympathy,
eschewing death and choosing life,
whence first creation came to be,
beginning with maternal Earth,
whose own self-love gave rise to Sky.
Those, joining in incestuous mirth,
the race of Titans brought forth cruelly.
Then came the fabled Age of Gold
when work and sickness were unknown,
goods were neither bought nor sold
and all men reaped, though none had sown.
Wise rulers faltered, fools took over,
each reign declining from the last,
for epigones aren't what their forbears were
and sequels seldom equal glories past.
But the fourth, the Heroic Age,
produced a race of men unrivaled
in vibrant strength, consummate courage,
and that's the idyl here unraveled.
Of Heracles' indomitable might,
proved in many an arduous trial
I sing, nor is the burden light
unless, dear Muse, you aid my toil.

Book I

Beginnings oft portend the end.
From little things we fathom great.
And what the Logos has ordained,
no verbal vandal can invalidate.
Amphitryon was off at war
when Zeus in thrice-prolongèd night,
disguised as him she waited for,
beguiled Alcmena of a husband's right.
When the real Amphitryon showed up,
his wife, whom Zeus had ridden hard,
said: "Don't you ever get enough?
Well, just don't take all night. I'm tired!"
When her confinement was at hand,
Zeus, beaming with a father's pride,
announced that child would rule the land
who next was born a purebred Perseid.
Then Hera, up to her old tricks,
said: "No doubt what you say is so,
but will you swear an oath by Styx?
Talk is cheap and words are wind, you know."
So Zeus took the irrevocable vow
and swore his words would come to pass,
then nodded his colossal brow,
mute witness to his giant ignorance.

Or so she thought, so Hera flew
to spur Nicippe's labor on,
although her infant wasn't due,
that he might reign instead of Zeus' son.
Eurystheus was born a king,
then Heracles and Iphicles, his brother;
twin sons born of a dual engendering;
one mortal, half divine the other.
But Hera's success didn't quench
her resentment. Quite the reverse.
It whetted her thirst for revenge

against Zeus and his half-breed papoose.
Twin serpents out of Hell's abyss
crept stealthily at her command,
gliding with surreptitious hiss
o'er barren soil and burning sand.
Slithering into the nursery,
they raised their pointy reptile heads.
Iphicles cried uncontrollably,
while Herc threw toys like hand-grenades.
The fanged assassins coiled to strike,
but Heracles, undaunted, stood his ground.
Alcmena entered and let out a shriek
to see her son in danger of a wound.
He gripped a snake in either fist
and squeezed so hard they couldn't breathe,
until they ceased to writhe and twist,
then dropped them lifeless to the floor beneath.

Amphitryon, stunned by the incident,
consulted the blind seer Teiresias,
who said the meaning of the portent
must be that Heracles Zeus' offspring was.
The prophet augured many things
the son of Zeus would undergo:
fierce wars, protracted wanderings,
and stubborn labors fraught with woe.
The child just smiled at their concern
with the insouciance of youth
as if he knew he'd one day earn
eternal fame for his immortal worth.
Amphitryon commenced with pride
to educate the growing boy
and showed how best the chariot to guide
in battle and his enemies destroy.
Autolycus taught the wrestling art,
the holds, maneuvers, and what not.
The disciple eclipsed the expert,
refining and adding as he went.
From Eurytus he conned the skill

of archery, the bowman's lethal craft,
till he could hit his prey at will
and mete out death with every shaft.
Swordsmanship he learned from Castor,
one of the swan-born Dioscuri,
and soon surpassed his fencing-master.
Even Pollux marveled at his fury.

Feeling the Muses were neglected,
Alcmena gleefully selected
a poet—vain perhaps, but gifted—
to teach her son. The boy objected.
The omniscient mom insisted,
chirping: "You'll thank me for it later."
The dutiful youngster yielded,
though it went against his nature.
The music master—named Linus,
had recently opened up shop.
He was half-brother to Orpheus
and a pretty hip dude for a fop.
When Alcides arrived—under protest—
Linus thought: "Not even my brother,
that wunderkind no woman can resist,
could do much with Li'l Abner here."
He handed Heracles a lyre.
It seemed a toy in his huge hands.
He showed him how to pluck the wire.
Heracles strummed the trembling strands.
To demonstrate, the poet sings.
The student patiently attended,
but accidentally broke one of the strings.
With that, the music lesson ended.
The poet dealt the lad a crease,
meant less to punish than correct.
Untutored in such niceties,
on him it had an adverse side-effect.

He brained the bard with his own lyre,
which made a most discordant noise.

Linus went to join the Muses' choir
and swell their number with his dulcet voice.
A trial was subsequently held.
Heracles was charged with murder.
The jury box by lot was filled.
The bailiff shouted: "Order, order!"
The upshot of the trial was this:
Heracles declared his innocence,
citing a law of Rhadamanthys
that pardoned killing in self-defense.
The jury found him innocent.
The judge approved the apophthegm:
"A man who turns to violence
will come to a violent end,"
and urged him to learn self-control,
then pardoned him on one condition
—which seemed to Heracles a trifle droll—
that he renounce his musical ambition.
Amphitryon owned flocks of sheep
that pastured on Mt. Cithaeron,
whose wooded slopes and rugged peaks
were home to wild boar, wolf and lion.
Heracles was sent to play shepherd
where his exuberance would do less harm
guarding against lion, fox and leopard,
and watching over the family farm.

It was the childhood of the year
when every insect, bird and flower,
and every leaf the branches wear
is rife with Aphrodite's ancient power.
An old prowler haunted this wood,
a lean, morose, remorseless beast,
and foraged in Alcides' neighborhood.
Many a lamb had been its midnight feast.
One day, the burly outdoorsman
stumbled on the feline felon
lashing its tail, shaking its tangled mane,
and gnawing on a hapless fawn.

Before he could pluck an arrow
and notch it on the taut bowstring,
the carnivore pounced on the hero,
claws bared, jaws wide and eyeballs glowing.
Grabbing the lion by the throat,
he wrung its neck like a pullet,
constricting his grip like a tourniquet
till he crushed its greedy gullet.
He flayed the deflated catamount,
devoting its pelt to the gods;
then, still dazed from the excitement,
began threading his way through the woods.
Along the footpath he followed,
beside a tree, there lay a well
whose water was sacred to Apollo.
Whoso drank, the future could foretell.

The hero paused awhile to rest
under the patriarchal laurel.
He took a drink to ease his thirst
and listened to a plaintive owl.
As he contemplated his fate,
two maids appeared before his eyes.
The first, named Pleasure, seemed to indicate
by looks and gestures, luxury and ease.
The second, Virtue, had a careworn air,
suggesting toil and a lasting name.
Both girls were superlatively fair,
but Heracles preferred enduring fame.
He still had many miles to travel,
so Heracles pursued his darkening way
till his eyes could scarce unravel
the path that seemed so clear by day.
Nestled snugly on Mt. Helicon
was a quaint hamlet called Thespiae.
Each spring to honor Venus' son,
the Thespians would dance and play.
To this town he now bent his step,
till he came upon the splendid home

of Thespius, the agèd king who kept
the laws and scepter, governing alone.

As Heracles approached the door,
two hounds beset him from the porch.
Curious what roused them at that hour,
a slender girl emerged bearing a torch.
"Don't be afraid," the hero said,
"for though these dogs think me a lion
come to prey on witless sheep, instead,
I'm just a hunter like Orion
who lost my way among the hills.
But tell me, isn't this the place
where Thespius, that gentle man, fulfills
the will of Zeus, dispensing justice?"
His easy manner calmed her fears.
"Kind stranger, you can stay the night
if Papa gives consent, who shares
this home with fifty daughters and a wife.
Indeed his name is Thespius and he
has ruled this city many years.
He treats the people like a father; they
revere and bless him in their prayers."
She led the way; he followed after
into the spacious domicile.
Once inside, a gust of girlish laughter
erupted from a chamber down the hall.
When Heracles entered the room,
the laughter ceased and all eyes turned.
To counteract the sudden gloom,
Thespius, in a cheery voice, intoned:

"By Zeus, this is a lucky sign,
for during this morning's sacrifice
the entrails presaged a divine
occurrence ere the moon rose twice.
Come in then; tell me who you are
and whence you came. But first relax.
It's obvious you've traveled far.

Eat first, then give me all the facts."
They laid a table for their guest
with food and darkly sparkling wine,
which Heracles consumed with zest,
the king and all his daughters looking on.
When he'd satisfied his hunger,
Alcides told the kindly king
about the poet slain in anger,
the trial, the lion; in short—everything.
The king was favorably impressed
by the manhood of the stranger,
his candor, strength and willingness
to encounter every kind of danger.
He thought: "He'd be the perfect sire
to procreate in Procris' bed."
But then he mused: "Why only her?
Why not give all my kids a kid?"
At last he said: "You must be tired.
Procris here will show you where to sleep."
But in his heart he secretly conspired
to make the young buck earn his keep.

She led her houseguest by the arm.
The room was dark as a moonless night.
He soon surrendered to her charm,
lost in the valley of love and delight.
The oldest, when the act was done,
excused herself to get some water.
The next girl entered, and so on,
till he made love to every daughter,
believing each to be the same
as she whom he had first embraced;
except the youngest, who refrained.
It ill became her years to be unchaste.
Each daughter gave birth to a son,
but though he only slept with forty-nine,
he fathered fifty-one children—
the first and last in line had twain.
We draw the curtain on our hero,

immersed in this steamy ordeal,
taking no thought for tomorrow,
a soldier on love's battlefield.

Book II

Genius can be grandiose and vain,
veering between God and devil.
Wisdom is Janus-like, a spinning coin
with virtue as the head and vice the tail.
When Dawn adorned herself in pink
and banished sleep from children's eyes,
Heracles, who barely slept a wink,
rose fresh from his nocturnal exercise.
Famished by his amorous labors,
he fared on what his host provided,
grateful for such generous neighbors,
and over all the jovial king presided.
He bid farewell to Thespius
and Helicon, the Muses' hill,
with some regret at parting thus
where he had been amused so well.
He met some heralds on the road
who boasted they were on the way
to collect the tribute Thebes owed,
and joked that if they didn't pay,
they'd lop off the ears and noses
of the townsfolk, so they'd be unable
to hear birdsong or savor roses,
which Heracles found reprehensible.

He seized the envoys—two brothers—
and did to them the very thing
they threatened to inflict on others,
jeering: "Take that tribute to your king!"
The king of Orchomenus fumed
to see his heralds mutilated
and fulminated Thebes was doomed
unless the culprit was extradited.
Creon, king of Thebes, was loath
to go to war for one man's fault.
Better to yank a rotten tooth
to spare the body grief, he thought.

Besides, the city had no arms,
for these were taken by the Minyans
when their army spoiled, like swarms
of locusts, Thebes and its environs.
But Heracles convinced the youth
to fight back like their ancestors,
and made them take a solemn oath
to choose death before surrender.
They made the rounds of all the temples
where spoils of war were dedicated
and found there many good examples
of former glory slightly antiquated.
When every new recruit was armed,
Alcides ranged the men in ranks.
Under his tutelage they learned
the art of fighting in phalanx.

Amid these martial preparations,
an oracle arrived from Delphi
predicting victory celebrations
if *the noblest* committed suicide.
There still lived in Thebes at that time
the scion of an ancient family tree;
a warrior—Antipoenus by name—
sprung from a dragon's tooth in Cadmus' day.
Opinion was unanimous:
the Delphic priestess had picked him.
But the old flint was adamant,
growling, "Find another victim!"
The daughters of the nobleman
were mortified by his reply
and, saying it referred to them,
leapt harum-scarum in the sea.
The town paid them every honor,
proclaiming if they won the war,
it was due to girlish valor
and not the soldiers' quaint armor.
The Minyan army had set out,
meanwhile, led by the king soi-même.

When this intelligence was brought
to Thebes, they knew it was showtime.
Alcides marshaled all his troops
and led them to a mountain pass
where numbers would be of little use
and a few repel attack en masse.

From atop this lofty plateau,
they had a panoramic view
of the Minyan army far below,
like insects moving to and fro.
When nightfall came, Alcides crept
among the unsuspecting enemy
and stole their horses as they slept,
then killed the flower of their chivalry.
Daylight revealed the brutal slaughter,
the littered corpses oozing life
as if a battle had been fought there,
a scene of bitterness and grief.
The customary rites were held
—the funeral pyre and burial urn—
before the army had dispelled
its pent-up grief and ceased to mourn.
Advancing up the mountainside,
the troops were eager for a fight,
to kill whoever swung the sword
that slew their friends that gruesome night.
As the host of Minyan soldiers
filed through a narrow débouché,
the Thebans greeted them with boulders
before springing their ambuscade.
Heracles plunged in the fracas
and cut down men like dumb cattle.
"Don't let that maniac attack us!"
they prayed, and many fled the battle.

Erginus tried to halt his men,
but they were deaf to his commands,

until at last he also turned and ran,
for safety oft on prudent flight depends.
Exulting in their victory,
Heracles' soldiers dogged the heels
of the retreating enemy,
showing no mercy to their appeals.
Marching at a rigorous pace
throughout the night, when morning broke,
the Thebans stood before the gates
of Orchomenus, as they had hoped.
They lost no time but went to work
and cut a tree to batter down
the doors, which splintered at the shock,
forcing their way inside the town.
Like a storm that fiercely rages
or like a swarm of angry bees
that neither prayers nor tears assuages,
the Thebans fought, urged on by Heracles.
Erginus led a stout resistance
but alas, the Thebans fought so well,
in desperation at this mischance,
he fled inside his palace citadel.
Amid this scene of death and ruin,
many brave soldiers met their end.
Among those killed was wise Amphitryon,
to Heracles a father and a friend.

Heracles was filled with malice
upon learning Amphitryon was dead
and flew like a hawk to the palace
to punish the author of the deed.
Erginus was seated on his throne
in full costume—robe, crown and scepter.
In an icy, triumphant tone,
he scowled: "So you are Thebes' defender!"
"Don't waste your breath on me old man,"
said Heracles. "A better man than you
has died this day and I don't give a damn
if I die or not, so long as you do!"

When Heracles held up Erginus'
freshly decapitated head,
the battlefield lapsed into silence
and the Minyans capitulated.
Heracles was hailed a savior,
gained new status, was raised in rank.
Forgotten was his past behavior.
The incident with Linus was a prank.
For his skill at martial slaughter,
his flair for taking human life,
King Creon gave his eldest daughter,
Megara, to become the strong man's wife.
The ceremony was barely over,
the hymn to Hymen scarcely sung,
the wedding guests only half sober,
the honeymoon hardly begun

when an ally of the Minyans,
King Pyraechmus of Euboea,
made what some, in their opinions,
called the worst mistake of his career.
He claimed the outcome of the war
had been a fluke, a quirk of fate,
the freak of some capricious star,
as his own campaign would demonstrate.
Once more Alcides took the field.
The fight was bitterly contested.
The enemy was forced to yield.
The reckless monarch was arrested.
The king was made an object lesson,
a warning to ambitious despots,
to discourage further aggression
and give the weary troops a respite.
He was tied between two horses.
At the signal they were driven.
Torn asunder by opposing forces,
the corpse no burial was given.
The war concluded, peace restored,
life's ageless tempo was resumed.

The poor worked hard for their reward,
the rich with profits were consumed.
Time went by, Alcides prospered.
Each passing year his family grew.
To his wife he spoke no cross word.
Their life seemed like a dream come true.

Hera, watching from Olympus,
—much has passed since she was last heard—
said: "My husband Zeus a pimp is,
pandering to his Boeotian bastard!
The royal satyr will be sorry.
He'll change his womanizing ways.
I'll send Tisiphone the Fury
the brain of Heracles to craze!"
She found the Fury in her cell,
mixing some foul-smelling potion
distilled from vermin bred in Hell
to sell to hags across the ocean.
To tell the story in detail
would take too long. The spell was cast.
The Fury worked her wicked will.
Alcides by a demon was possessed.
His children practiced side by side
with the sons of Iphicles, his brother,
performing feats of arms, learning to ride,
sharpening their martial skills together.
To Heracles' disordered mind,
his sons and nephews were marauders
coming to steal the Thebans blind
and carry off their wives and daughters.
The hero, lunging with his spear,
grazed his favorite nephew, Iolaus
who, being agile, managed to leap clear
and shouted: "Uncle wants to slay us!"

Taking aim with bow and arrows,
he better compassed his desire,

shot them down like helpless sparrows
and cast their bodies in the fire.
When he perceived his grievous error,
the heinous nature of his crime,
his mind was overcome with horror,
his heart was overwhelmed with shame.
Lamenting what his hands had done,
his shrill cries scarified the air.
He shunned the comfort of the sun,
stunned by the blackjack of despair.
When time diminished his distress
and reconciled him to his plight,
he sought the home of old King Thespius,
well versed in every cleansing rite.
For kindred murder he was purified.
A lamb was led in by a halter.
The gods were asked to intercede.
Its blood was sprinkled on the altar.
Thespius suggested he go
consult the Delphic oracle.
His fate the prophetess would show,
babbling in a voice hysterical.
The priestess was a wizened crone
who'd been a virgin all her life.
To her alone were all things known.
Kings staked their crowns on her advice.

As Heracles approached the fane
to learn what fortune held in store,
the priestess and her menial train
were shuffling out the temple door.
The priestess muttered: "Who are you?"
He: "You're the priestess, don't you know?"
"The past and future, yes, it's true.
The present is a little harder though.
Be a treasure, give me a clue."
He: "My name is Heracles of Thebes."
"Mix lamb and tortoise in a stew.
It's one of my home remedies."

After much pointless dialogue,
which we often find in fiction,
the priestess, in a foreign brogue,
made the following prediction:
"Twelve years of labor to complete
in service to a worthless king,
twelve labors great in cold and heat
and many more in war and wandering
till, spent with toil and travail hard,
and travels far by land and sea,
the gods your efforts will reward
with boundless fame and immortality."
With that, the priestess was exhausted
and sank unconscious to the ground.
Feeling his time not wholly wasted,
Alcides hitched a ride back into town.

Book III

Nothing galls the human spirit,
defiant in its natural pride
and conscious of superior merit
like serving one to whom it's denied.
Some authors contend Heracles
suffered symptoms of depression
like Plato and his mentor Socrates,
a common ailment in uncommon men.
In any case, feeling despondent
at what the oracle foretold
and at the melancholy prospect
of serving one who couldn't hold
a candle to him in love or war,
he moved to Tiryns, the city
where he was born and reared and where
Eurystheus enjoyed sole sovereignty.
He generated quite a stir
returning to his native town.
His military exploits were
a favorite theme for miles around.
Eurystheus noted with disgust
his cousin's triumphant arrival
and grew increasingly jealous,
seeing in him a dangerous rival.

When Heracles informed the king
he'd come to Tiryns to atone
for kindred murder by doing
any ten tasks he wanted done,
Eurystheus' eyes began to gleam.
That night, he lay awake in bed
concocting a diabolical scheme
to get rid of Heracles for good.
Whether by Typhon and Echidna
the Nemean lion was begotten,
or by Orthrus and the Chimera,
time's bookkeepers have forgotten.

The lion was extremely fierce,
a ravenous and savage creature
with a hide no man-made blade could pierce,
ergo impregnable by nature.
The first task Eurystheus set
was to exterminate this menace.
He had no choice but to accept,
so Heracles struck out at once.
Tramping the dusty road to Argos
with bow and arrows, club and sword,
he met a shepherd named Molorchus
whose son the lion had devoured.
He asked Alcides if he'd care
to stay the night, as it was late.
They dined on coarse and simple fare,
and both men relished every bite.

Next day Molorchus went to offer
a calf to Hera, but Alcides
bid him not to harm the heifer,
but wait instead for thirty days.
He said: "If I return within
that time, we'll sacrifice to Zeus.
If I don't make it back by then,
to me as demigod address your vows."
Reaching Nemea around midday,
he looked in vain for sight or sound,
or someone to direct the way
to where the lion might be found.
After a long and fruitless search,
he spied the lion just returning
from another bloody debauch,
for it had killed again that morning.
The son of Zeus swiftly unleashed
some arrows with unerring skill.
They bounded harmless from the beast,
which merely scratched and switched its tail.
Next, he unsheathed his trusty sword
and tried to run the lion through.

It yawned as if completely bored
as the faultless falchion snapped in two.
Grasping the haft of his olive club,
he brought it down on the lion's skull.
It shattered with a resounding thud.
The club, that is; the lion found it dull.

The feline, to escape the heat,
sought refuge in a cave nearby.
Heracles, to forestall retreat,
sealed off one entrance with debris.
Then, following the lion's path
—the cave, you see, was open-ended—
he goaded it to savage wrath
by grappling with it empty-handed.
There was no turning back. The cat
was out of the bag, so he fought,
for he'd learned to exploit the hate
and rage that augmented his might.
He crooked an arm around its neck
in a chokehold, catch as catch can,
bearing down till he felt it crack.
The cat went slack from lack of oxygen.
Returning with the lion's carcass
across his neck, by the same road
as before, he found pious Molorchus
worshiping *Herakles* the demigod.
The shepherd trembled like a leaf,
astonished at the lion's size.
When he'd overcome his disbelief,
to Zeus the two men sacrificed.
From then on, the Nemean games
were held to honor Father Zeus,
while one who died a babe in arms,
Opheltes' laurels fell into disuse.

That evening they celebrated
and drank a jar of Chian wine.

The old man sang and danced, elated,
and struck the cat that ate his son.
At daybreak, Heracles ventured out
to hew a new club from an olive tree.
If the sun hit him just right, he might
have passed for some sylvan deity.
When news of Heracles' approach
was bruited in the marketplace,
the folks of Tiryns crowded close
to touch the victim of the chase.
Many, however, were so scared
when they beheld the lion's scowl
that quite a number never dared.
Some even swore they heard it growl.
He led them through the city gates,
pied-piping through the market square;
setting the crowd a breathless pace,
they followed up the palace stair.
The king appeared, fearing disaster,
to quell the uproar at its source,
but stumbled, falling on his keister.
From there things went from bad to worse.
Lying supine, he looked aside
and saw the lion gazing back.
The last sound Eurystheus heard
was laughter as the sky went black.

The king eventually revived
and ordered Heracles in future,
if a like occasion should arise,
outside the gates display his capture.
No need to further embellish
tales everybody knows. It's said
Alcides felt a certain relish
seeing Eurystheus discomfited.
To Heracles it seemed a sin
to throw away the lion's pelt.
The question was how best to skin
the beast and so avoid the fault.

Thus, applying Occam's razor
and passing from effect to cause,
he found the only way to flay her
was with her own serrated claws.
Wearing its pelt for protection
made him impervious to attack
from arrows, spears—most any weapon.
For a helm he left the skull intact.
Saying no offense was taken,
the king let on that he was pleased,
but inwardly his mind was shaken,
exhibiting psychotic tendencies.
He had a blacksmith cast an urn
of bronze to bury in the earth.
On news of Heracles' return,
he hid within, provoking mirth.

Laughter is difficult to bear
when we're its involuntary cause.
This humor made the ruler swear
to get revenge whate'er the cost.
Eurystheus cast his mind about
for a task so risky to complete
as to leave the hero no way out
and end in imminent defeat.
It happens that in ancient Greece
there lived a plethora of pests
that gave the populace no peace
and sent her heroes forth on quests.
Such was the detested Hydra,
a killer snake with an ennead
of heads that stalked the swamps of Lerna
and filled its denizens with dread.
A courier was then dispatched
to carry Heracles a scroll
to which a letter was attached
explaining everything in full.
The journey only takes a day
to Lerna, but to vary it,

he picked up Iolaus on the way.
His nephew drove their chariot.
The road meanders by the coast
and, winding, wanders lazily
along. The cheerful eye is lost
in wonder gazing at a beryl sea.

Halting beside a sacred grove,
they turned the horses out to graze,
to crop wildflowers as they roved,
switching their tails to swat the flies.
The allies searched together till
Alcides spied the Hydra's den,
a fissure in a grassy knoll
beside a spring that bubbled from the fen.
Drawing a bead on its burrow,
he coaxed the monster from its lair
by firing a flaming arrow,
followed swiftly by several more.
The Hydra slowly issued forth.
It seemed a thing of vast extent.
Only a fiend could have given birth
to a beast so vile and virulent.
Eight smaller snakes around a stalk
—the mother stem was fertile—
writhed constantly, prepared to strike.
The main head was gold, ergo immortal.
It surged with a rippling motion,
curved fangs dripping toxic venom,
undulating like the ocean,
not side to side like lesser vermin.
Advancing through the underbrush,
the Hydra left a sticky spoor,
which Heracles was loath to touch,
its stench too potent to ignore.

As he drew close, it grew more fierce,
for he was no snake charmer.

The snakelets struck but couldn't pierce
the lion cape he wore for armor.
Wielding his club, Alcides rushed
to clout them at a frenzied pace,
but for every sentry snake he crushed,
two new ones sprouted in its place.
The Hydra coiled around his feet
to try and gain the upper hand.
The son of Zeus began to sweat,
for now he found it hard to stand.
As if not already hard put,
Crabzilla clambered from the swamp
and grabbed Alcides by the foot,
locking its huge claw like a clamp.
Crushing its shell with one deft stroke,
he reprimanded his nephew:
"This is no time to stand and gawk!
Shake a leg! Your Uncle needs you!"
Setting a patch of woods alight,
Iolaus fetched burning brands.
Whenever Heracles would smite
a snake, he seared the dangling strands.
Having subdued the lesser threat,
he used a golden sword to lop
the deathless head, which hissed and spit,
and stuffed it under a massive rock.

Its golden head safely buried,
he slit the Hydra's body wide
and dipped his arrows in its blood.
The viscous fluid quickly dried.
Zeus, watching from his recliner,
remarked, much to Hera's chagrin:
"What happened to your pet, my dear?
It seems my son made sushi of him."
Hera, flushed with indignation,
enshrined the crab in outer space,
raising it to a constellation
to reward its selfless sacrifice.

Book IV

Whether hind or boar or Holy Grail,
whatever flees as we pursue
becomes the symbol of mankind's ideal,
the good, the beautiful and true,
some lovely form we long to clasp
which, keeping steadily in view,
in spite of all eludes our grasp,
forever flies while we the chase renew.
Because he found him hard to kill,
Eurystheus esteemed it best
to keep him far away as possible
and send him deep into the wilderness.
The labor he was next assigned
his wit and matchless prowess proves:
to catch the Cerynean Hind,
a deer with golden horns and brazen hooves.
Some call it hart and others stag,
while some think no such thing exists.
Some say it only lives in the imag-
ination or the dreams of poets.
How Heracles pursued the hind
and chased it over Hell's half-acre
is what now occupies my mind.
Muse, help me cheat the undertaker.

Heracles began his distant quest
in Arcadia when snowdrifts form,
in a virgin forest in the midst
of a land known for its rustic charm.
The natives there wore sheepskin coats.
Rude huts kept out both heat and cold.
Instead of meat, they ate assorted nuts
and seeds, as did their patriarchs of old.
The hind haunted a certain hill
frequented by the goddess Artemis.
Around its base there flowed a rill

noteworthy for its pristine loveliness.
After a week of silent waiting,
nothing of moment had occurred
except the musical complaining
of one lonely goliardic bird.
Ten days the holy spot was guarded
but still no sign was seen or heard.
Small animals came and departed;
the son of Zeus was undeterred.
At last his patience was rewarded:
the sacred hind majestically appeared.
Its antlers had a roseate glow
like hot embers trapped in amber.
The stag seemed ghostlike in the snow,
its coat like puréed alabaster.
To avoid offending Artemis
and capture the elusive deer
without excessive use of force,
he tracked it for an entire year,

    through raging rivers, woods and lakes,
past thorns and thickets, heath and pond,
o'er bush and brier, bogs and brakes,
to the land beyond the cold north wind.
Through deep ravine and level plain,
the hind became his cynosure;
field and fountain, moor and mountain,
he followed it like a guiding star.
After a year, the deer grew weary
and so, as though bored with the game,
sought its mountain sanctuary,
returning to familiar haunts again.
Descending to the river Ladon,
the creature made as if to cross
but, as it was about to wade in,
seemed too good a target to let pass.
Heracles let fly an arrow,
pinning its forelegs where it stood.
The shaft bisected bone and sinew

and never drew a drop of blood.
He hastened through Arcadia
with the hind across his shoulders
to beef up the king's regalia
and awe his fawning courtiers.
Artemis met him on his journey
when he crossed Mycenae's border.
She: "I hope you have a good attorney."
He: "I was just obeying orders."

The beauty poets eulogize
was manifest—the word made flesh.
Only a fool with two glass eyes
could miss the meaning of that text.
The virgin huntress made him swear
that upon completion of his quest,
he'd treat her holy beast with care
and return it unscathed to the forest.
The man of iron kept his word.
When all had gandered at the deer,
the animal was readily restored
with only minor wear and tear.
Eurystheus had hatched a plot,
meanwhile, to put him in harm's way
and end his labors or, if not,
to catch a still more deadly prey.
There was a boar that used to ravage
crops and fields near Erymanthus
and caused considerable damage.
Its huge tusks made it doubly dangerous.
Ordered to bring it back alive,
the son of Zeus set out forthwith,
but not before he bought supplies
and paid a visit to the village smith.
Criminals had a verve back then
absent in today's banausic crooks.
Lacking humor was more inhuman
than murder in their code of ethics.

Termerus was an arrant rascal
who used to challenge passersby
to butt heads with him billy style,
killing those who dared to disobey.
As Heracles casually proceeded
toward Erymanthus and its boar,
he found his progress was impeded
by a blackguard with a jagged scar.
"Whither so fast my friend? Such haste!
Haven't you heard that every man
must come to the same end at last?
Why waste the day? Live while you can!"
Thinking he would easily dispose
of him, Termerus explained the rules.
Then, glowering beneath their brows,
they squared off like a pair of bulls
to try the merit of their cause
and test the temper of their skulls.
Alcides' density was greater,
for though the felon's head was big,
he crushed it when they rushed together
like a ripe melon or rotten egg.
A band of Centaurs lived nearby,
a race intractable and proud
who traced their lineage to the sky,
a man's infatuation with a cloud.
Pholus, of all the Centaur breed,
was kindest and most generous.
When some weary wayfarer applied
for refuge, he'd always acquiesce.

When Heracles stopped by his cave,
Pholus welcomed his famous guest.
Coaxing the embers into a blaze,
he offered to share his meager feast.
He'd recently butchered a sheep

and took some mutton from a shelf.
For Heracles he cooked the meat
but preferred to eat it raw himself.
Pholus drily observed: "I guess
you met Termerus. Queer fellow that."
And Heracles replied: "Why yes,
we had a pleasant little *tête-à-tête*."
The reader understands, of course,
that Heracles did not speak French,
but what's the use of writing verse
if what we say makes perfect sense?
When man and Centaur ate their fill,
Alcides looked about for wine,
for wine with meals is indispensable
to lift the hearts of those who dine.
The Centaur eyed him cautiously
until the son of Zeus burst out:
"This is a damn fine hostelry!
Is there no wine to end this drought?"
At this, Pholus recalled the jar
the wine god, Dionysus, gave
to a Centaur many years before,
who buried it inside the cave.

The drunken god's instructions were,
against the inevitable day,
to save the jar of choice liqueur
till Heracles should come to stay.
When Pholus broke the bottle's seal,
ambrosial odors filled the room.
The evening breeze broadcast the smell,
infusing the air with its rich perfume.
The Centaurs soon became aware
that wine was wafted on the breeze
and gathered to demand a share,
brandishing axes, rocks, uprooted trees.
Mild-mannered Pholus was afraid
and would have granted their demands,

but Heracles was undismayed,
repulsing them with flaming brands.
The first assailants to be killed
were headstrong Ancius and Agrius.
Two more by poison shafts were felled
whose names were Oreus and Hylaeus.
The others fled to Malea's cliffs
where Chiron lived in solitude
since the battle with the Lapiths
drove him from his previous abode.
Chiron was their tacit ruler.
Skilled in physic and philosophy,
he sometimes acted as a tutor
to noble youths of marked ability.

But safe asylum proved elusive.
Alcides found them in a rage,
complaining loudly of ill usage
and cowering about their agèd sage.
The Centaurs scattered like a shot
when Heracles stepped into view.
His bowstring gave a soft report
as a wingèd shaft leapt from the bow.
Passing through Elatus's arm,
the arrow lodged in Chiron's knee.
The hero watched in stunned alarm
as the old healer howled in agony.
Alcides was beside himself
and hurried to remove the shaft.
He dressed the wound with Chiron's help,
using his most effective salve.
Retiring in anguish to his cell,
Chiron nursed his wound—to no avail.
The arrow bore the Hydra's gall;
no balm could coax the sore to heal.
Whether it was the constant pain
or that eternal life grew onerous,
he sought to leave the world—in vain,
till aided by profound Prometheus.

The Titan offered, it is said,
to take the ailing Centaur's place
and be immortal in his stead.
Thus Chiron died, the wisest of his race.

Pholus, remaining at the cave,
where he hid from the hostilities,
was about to dig a fitting grave
to house his fallen relatives.
He found an arrow on the ground
where Hylaeus lay in the dust
and wondered how so small a wound
could kill a creature so robust.
He handled it too carelessly,
dropping it on his hairy fetlock.
The poison acted instantly,
striking him lifeless on the spot.
When Heracles came on the scene,
he wept at the unforeseen event
and realized he was to blame
for gentle Pholus' fatal accident.
He washed the body in a stream
and buried him at the ascent
to the lofty peak that bears his name.[1]
The mountain was his monument.
Now Heracles set out once more,
resolved, whatever fate might bring,
to catch the misbehaving boar
and lead it captive to a craven king.
To trap the boar involved some risks
for, if attacked while it was fresh,
he'd be in danger from its tusks
and, if too forceful, he'd cause its death.

Fresh powder blanketed the earth.
Its tracks were easy to discern
and pointed to some heavy undergrowth.
Alcides followed in the icy dawn.
Giving his most ferocious yell,

he flushed it from its thorny brake.
It took off like a mortar shell,
trailing clouds of rubbish in its wake.
Bounding across snow-covered plains,
the wild hog petered out at length.
He bound the animal in chains
before it could regain its strength.
Heracles ferried his feral freight
piggyback like a tun of lard,
dropping it off at the palace gate,
while Eurystheus cowered in his jar.

Book V

Our joys are seldom unalloyed.
Some bitter clings to every sweet.
Cruel thorns by roses are deployed.
Love is often followed by regret.
After the death of King Cretheus,
Aeson, his son, took the throne,
which nettled his half-brother Pelias,
for the villain had plans of his own.
He imprisoned Aeson and scorned him
and, to add spice to the scandal,
a menacing oracle warned him:
Beware of a lad with one sandal.
When Jason showed up—you guessed it,
he only had one of his shoes.
While crossing the river he lost it.
It got stuck in alluvial ooze.
The rascal asked: "Who are you son?"
He answered: "My pals call me Jason,
but back in the town where I'm from,
Diomedes I'm hailed, son of Aeson."
Aware of the evil he wrought,
he sought for a way to inveigle
the son of his rival. He thought:
"I'll clip the wings of this eagle."

He tricked him into leaving home
and sent him on a wild goose chase
by vowing he'd renounce the throne
if Jason fetched the Golden Fleece.
That's why the heroes assembled
from the furthest corners of Greece,
and why the sea, earth and sky trembled
—on account of a moth-eaten fleece.
Heracles joined the Argo's crew,
seasoned warriors one and all,

while Hylas came to guard his bow
and be his harlequin in general.
Hylas was an affable youth.
Stars scintillated in his eyes.
His ringlets fell pell mell, his breath
was sweet as horehound lozenges.
Heracles killed Hylas' father.
The rogue fell afoul of his club
in a quarrel several years before.
He adopted the orphaned cub.
Before embarking on their mission,
the other men saw fit to offer
to let him lead the expedition,
but Heracles declined the honor,
and he advised, to fend off rancor,
the crew give Jason their devotion.
It was agreed; the ship weighed anchor
and cut a passage through the ocean.

The sailors landed at the isle
of Lemnos, ruled by lonely whores—
a delicate and daunting trial
for a virile band of horny tars!
They decided to relax awhile
to sample life on foreign shores,
and got the womenfolk with child
before returning to their oars.
After hitching up their trousers,
the chieftains put to sea again.
They manned the oars and loosed the hawsers.
The taut sheets bellied in the wind.
Passing the Hellespont by night,
they left the Aegean heading east.
Keeping the mainland on the right,
the vessel hugged the Phrygian coast.
By dinnertime the ship had come,
by dint of many sleepless hours,
within a bowshot of Mt. Dindymum,
also known as the Mount of Bears.

In the shadow of the mountain,
the Doliones built their city.
By means of cattle, wine and grain,
they led a life of gay simplicity.
King Cyzicus, the city's ruler,
had just been joined in matrimony
to a girl as fresh as any flower,
a princess of distinguished ancestry.

The newlyweds were drunk on love
and planned to end their days together.
In each heart an equal passion strove;
she was beautiful and he was clever.
Coming ashore, the Argonauts
were given a warm reception
and set aside all solemn thoughts
to join the nuptial celebration.
In those days on the Mount of Bears
there lived a host of earth-born giants
boasting six hands apiece—three pairs—
a feat unknown to modern science.
Amid the gaiety and revels,
as cakes and ale were going round,
these overgrown, six-handed devils
descended on the unsuspecting town.
Chaos ensued. In their alarm,
mothers ran to seek their children.
The old and infirm fled from harm,
while others found the scene bewildering.
Seizing a spear that stood nearby,
Alcides hurled it with such force,
it pierced one giant through the eye
and laid him sprawling on the grass.
Grabbing his legendary bow,
he shot an ogress in the breast,
for there were lady giants too,
equally savage and grotesque.

The monsters lobbed great, jagged rocks
and tore huge trees up by the root.
The mountain echoed with the shrieks
of people being trampled underfoot.
Taking their cue from Heracles,
the other heroes followed suit
and ran to meet the fearsome freaks
as Jason raised the battle shout.
The fight was fiercely contested.
The giants' might was impressive,
but when the dust had subsided,
Greek derring-do proved decisive.
The monsters were annihilated.
The city once again was free.
The heroes were congratulated,
having won without one casualty.
They laid the ogres side by side
like railroad ties along the beach.
As they putrefied in the tide,
crustaceans feasted on their flesh.
Leading a festive entourage,
the effervescent bride and groom
bid their visitors a bon voyage
and eagerly resumed their honeymoon.
A placid breeze mildly propelled
the Argo forward on its course,
until a sudden thunder-squall assailed
the ship with gales of staggering force.

The ship was helpless as a toy,
tossed to and fro as if in play
to entertain some thoughtless boy
who magnifies a puddle to a sea.
At last they came upon an island
and seized the offer chance extended
to plant their feet once more on dry land
and lie low till the tempest ended.

As they began to disembark,
they met with yet another threat:
bandits attacked them in the dark.
They had no choice but to retaliate.
They put the buccaneers to flight,
killing some and wounding others.
Daylight revealed their tragic plight,
proving that sorrow waits on lovers.
King Cyzicus lay pale as snow,
surrounded by a pool of blood.
Jason's spear delivered the blow
and Atropos severed life's thread.
Ironically, the ship was driven,
conditions being what they were,
right back to its place of origin,
arriving on an unfamiliar shore.
The Doliones, seeing the ship,
thought it carried armed invaders
coming to plunder, rob and rape,
and gathered to repel the raiders.

When Cleite heard the woeful tidings
—for that was his lovely spouse's name—
she cried: "Now I believe those writings
that say the gods don't give a damn!"
Using a bedsheet for a noose,
she tied it to a roof timber,
moving with unswerving purpose
like a revenant or sleepwalker.
Then, cinching the end that hung loose
snugly around her lissome neck,
she went to join her darling Cyzicus,
giving the chair one final, fatal kick.
The nymphs of the surrounding wood,
heartbroken by these sad affairs,
wept so profusely, long and hard,
a fountain sprouted from their tears.
The pair were buried near their home
where traces of the barrow still appear.

The heroes slowly paced around the tomb
armed cap-à-pie in burnished battle gear.
Funeral games were celebrated
with sports of the customary sort.
All the Argonauts competed
except Heracles, who stood apart.
A tempest raged for days on end,
preventing the crew from sailing.
They implored the gods to relent,
but their prayers were unavailing.

One night as Jason snored in bed,
the sleeping chief received a sign:
a halcyon fluttered o'er his head
and warbled an ecstatic strain.
Mopsus, who was a learned seer
and knew the language of the birds,
just happened to be standing near
and interpreted its cryptic chirps.
He roused the slumbering leader
and lulled him with a dull recital
whose tedium would bore the reader
and make a blasé poet suicidal.
The offended powers were appeased,
turning the world a gracious mien.
Counsel prevailed, contention ceased.
Universal justice reigned supreme.
Leaving behind the dismal scene,
sleek Argo slipped away from shore.
As for the doleful king and queen,
the Doliones wept a whole month more.
The crew was acting so downcast,
depressed by what had taken place,
the son of Zeus spoke up at last
and rallied them in a cheerful voice.
"What happened to that young couple
is unfortunate, but life goes on.
At least they'll never know the trouble
of old age. Their worries are done.

Circumstance conspired to ruin
the games, for it seemed disrespectful
to vie for prizes like children
when we were partly responsible.
But now, lest any doubt who's strongest
or boast in jest I'm past my prime,
let's find out who can row the longest.
The last to ship his oar wins our esteem."
The Argo was a marvelous craft.
Her prow was carved from a sacred oak.
As they put their backs into the task,
the figurehead called out the stroke.
Orpheus kept time with his lyre,
who taught insensate stones to move.
Hylas joined in too, whose vocal fire
could melt the coldest heart with love.
The virile heroes rowed for hours
before their strength began to wane,
and little wonder. So would yours,
unless you fancy you're immune to pain.
The sun was dipping in the west
to pasture his sky-footed team
among the Islands of the Blest
and take a bath in Ocean Stream.
But ere his cresset was extinguished,
engulfed in clouds of mist and steam,
most of the sailors had relinquished
the right to boast themselves supreme.

Four rugged souls still tugged an oar:
Alcmena's son, great-hearted Heracles,
well-knit Jason, horse-loving Castor,
and his twin, godlike Polydeuces.
Castor's strength began to waver,
but he was determined to persist
till, shipping his own oar as a favor,
Polydeuces induced him to desist.
That left Heracles and Jason.

Seated across from each other,
both men labored at their station,
pulling the ship along together.
Alcides' strength could be compared
to some piston-driven mechanism.
A diesel engine would have fared
badly next to his impressive frame.
Despite his charisma and grace
and a form Apelles might have painted,
the competition proved too arduous
and, dropping his oar, Jason fainted.
At the same instant Jason fell,
tumbling clumsily in the aisle,
Heracles gave a strenuous pull,
snapping his oar like a pretzel.
The sailors, needing no command,
plied their oars with grim tenacity
until they reached the verdant strand
where the river Chius met the sea.

As the crew bivouacked for the night,
their boasting was replaced by groans.
They gathered wood in the fading light
and spoke in low, crepuscular tones.
With only one thing on his mind
—to make a more trustworthy oar—
Alcides left the Argonauts behind
and went to find the perfect fir.
If you traversed the land of Hellas
or the whole world for that matter,
you'd never find the likes of Hylas.
For comeliness there was none better.
Telling the rest: "I'll see you fellas!"
the lad set out in search of water.
Before long he observed a spring
encircled by soft grass and flowers
where nymphs oft came a-caroling
and danced away the playful hours.
Dryope that night had come to dwell

beneath the water's crystal firmament.
As Hylas knelt beside the pool,
the moon looked on in bored astonishment.
Pulling him beneath the surface,
she clasped him in a strict embrace.
Hylas was wildly alarmed at first,
but soon surrendered to her kiss.
Returning with his makeshift oar,
Heracles met Polyphemus.
Though the latter was his senior,
the former was far more famous.

"As I was strolling in the wood,"
Polyphemus stammered, "I heard a yell.
I ran to bring what help I could
and found Hylas' ewer by the well."
In a flurry of confused alarm,
they searched the surrounding terrain,
while from the bottom of the tarn,
Hylas watched, but not without a pang.
The son of Zeus was so distraught,
he charged all he met with to inquire
till the man or animal was caught
that brought harm to his darling squire.
Next morning they were miles away,
still vainly seeking Hylas' trail.
After waiting for them half a day,
the captain passed the word to sail.
Jason retrieved the Golden Fleece
with help from King Aeëtes' daughter.
His manners charmed the sorceress,
but their marriage ended in disaster.
The couple had a nasty quarrel,
for though he was a model sailor
and his wife Medea *was* immoral,
as a husband he was still a failure.

Book VI

Those who rely solely on force
to carry out some grand design
will have occasion for remorse.
Let subtlety and strength combine.
Some folks think Heracles an oaf
with less intelligence than brawn,
but many of his deeds give proof
of a restless and inventive brain.
Augeas held the throne of Elis,
a man of unrestrained ambition.
He styled himself a son of Helios
and feigned a sunny disposition.
The king was quite a cattle baron.
In fact, he owned so many head,
their number was hard to determine,
for every day they calved and bred.
Now cows are adept at alchemy
(for this we don't account them wiser);
by black arts they transmogrify
plain grass into cheap fertilizer.
This *dark matter* had accumulated
in such astonishing profusion,
the cattle stalls were inundated.
There was barely room to moo in.

Eurystheus smirked with furtive glee
to picture Heracles befouled with dung
and reveled in the vile indignity
he'd suffer ere the dirty work were done.
He ordered Heracles to Elis
to clean the stable in a day.
Smug at first, the king grew jealous
as the hero calmly strode away.
Alcides met an ancient swain
who eked a living from the soil.
The farmer looked as tough as whang,
his carcass jerked by years of toil.

The hero said: "Good day grandfather!
You seem familiar with these parts.
Tell me, if it isn't too much bother,
do you know King Augeas' whereabouts?"
The codger quit what he was doing
just long enough to wipe his brow,
then patiently resumed his hoeing,
determined to complete another row.
The old coot curtly said: "I should,
I called him boss for thirty years,
tending his cows and riding herd,
till I got too old to wrassle steers."
He stiffly laid aside his hoe
—for countryfolk are curious—
and led the way without further ado,
though his courtesy was spurious.

He kept his questions to himself,
but wondered at the stranger's garb.
Clad in a shaggy lion's pelt,
his right hand grasped a massive club.
Before the duo came in sight,
Augeas' dogs picked up their scent
and rushed at Heracles from every side;
nor was his seedy sidekick exempt.
By reaching down to pick up rocks
and talking gruff, the sly old timer
had done enough to cow the dogs
and tranquilize their katzenjammer.
"A dog's a rude, uncouth critter,"
he yokelized, "an empty blusterer,
but they'd be honored evermore
if they could sniff out character."
When Heracles and his companion
arrived at the sprawling estate,
cattle were streaming from the canyon
where they often went to ruminate.
Phoebus had finished his cosmic course
and parked his celestial calèche.

He put a nosebag on each horse
and fêted them with ambrosial mash.
But ere his dwindling light was spent,
Alcides hailed the haughty sovereign
and offered, for a small emolument,[2]
to clean the cowshed in one afternoon.

The king thought Heracles an oaf,
but saw no harm in playing along,
so he made him take a solemn oath
in front of Phyleus, his eldest son.
Augeas owned twelve spotless bulls,
groomed for their gallant services.
By far the most belligerent of these
was Phaeton, terror of all carnivores.
As they concluded their agreement,
the huge bull spied the lion pelt
that was Alcides' favorite garment
and charged the son of Zeus full tilt.
The hero met the charge head on
with no apparent sign of fear.
Seizing the angry bull's left horn,
he stopped it cold in mid-career.
The florid monarch was nonplussed
by this impromptu tour de force.
He tried to pass it off as just
bravado but it spooked him nonetheless.
Next morning at the rooster's shrill
charivari, its rustic reveille,
Heracles bashed a commodious hole
in the barn wall with his shillelagh.
The river Alpheus flowed close by
and bathed the meadows with its flood.
It was a cheap and plentiful supply
of water for the entire neighborhood.

Removing one of the giant doors
that opened into the spacious byre,

Alcides carried the gate perforce
and laid it athwart the river floor.
Once the river was obstructed,
the water sought another channel
and flowed as gravity directed,
cleansing the stable of its offal.
One Copreus, whose name means filth,
worked for the king in twin capacities,
and won more wealth by stealth than tilth,
unearthing libelous obscenities.
By plying him with gold and lies,
he wormed the truth from the old timer,
the gossip told him by his cronies,
though *he* put no stock in such a rumor.
Thus Copreus informed Augeas
that Heracles deserved no fee,
but was ordered by Eurystheus
to clean the cattle stalls for free.
The case was brought before a judge.
Phyleus was called to testify.
He bore the son of Zeus no grudge
and told the truth—his father swore to pay.
The ruddy tyrant fulminated
against his son's ill-timed apostasy.
He bellowed, sputtered, foamed and execrated,
and ranted in an apoplectic way.

The ruling on the suit was mooted.
Augeas sent them both packing.
Heracles withdrew and brooded.
Incentives to revenge weren't lacking.
He took fond leave of Phyleus
on the outskirts of Dulichium
and continued toward Olenus
where he slew the Centaur Eurytion.
Olenus' king, it seems, was guilty
of some careless indiscretion
to which the Centaur was a party
and vowed to publish his transgression.

The frantic king, to buy his silence,
agreed to his vulgar proposal:
his daughter's hand! She bid defiance,
being loath to such a gross betrothal.
On being informed how matters stood,
Alcides said: "Leave this to me."
He hid on a lonely stretch of road
and waited for the Centaur to prance by.
Eurytion came to fetch his bride,
but Heracles ambushed and slew him.
You could hardly call it homicide,
for Centaurs aren't completely human.
Eurystheus, true to character,
declared the labor of the stable
null and void, as it was done for hire,
which Heracles found unforgivable.

After exchanging bitter words,
Alcides traveled to Arcadia
to oust a host of noxious birds
wreaking havoc in the area.
Stymphalian Birds! What could be better
to test the mettle of our hero?
They'd impale you with a brazen feather
as deftly as a marksman's arrow.
They ate the weanlings of the flocks
and skewered farmers on their beaks,
then spewed their feces on the crops
so nothing green would grow for weeks.
They migrated from Wolves' Ravine
to flee those heartless predators
and settled under Mt. Cyllene
on Lake Stymphalus' headwaters.
Upon arriving at the marsh,
strange noises struck Alcides' ear.
The birds' discordant cries were harsh,
their grating voices terrible to hear.
The sodden turf was far too soft
to support a traveler on foot,

nor was the water deep enough
to keep a shallow skiff afloat.
His bow was useless at this juncture
to dislodge the pertinacious fowl,
for though he could've made a puncture
in some, he couldn't shoot them all.

The son of Zeus, never at a loss,
resorted to a cunning artifice.
He made a rattle out of brass,
a noisy sort of anti-bird device.
Climbing atop a rugged spur
that jutted from the mountainside,
he shook the sistrum with such verve,
it reverberated far and wide.
The birds, affrighted by the din,
dispersed in terror and confusion
and never bothered anyone again,
made timid by a nervous constitution.
Grant me, O Muse, in future chapters,
if I haven't croaked or been trepanned,
to send my readers into raptures
with some death-defying sleight of hand.

Book VII

Many a man who was a paragon
of wisdom crossed by stern adversity
has acted dumber than a stone
when overcome by sweet prosperity.
King Minos ruled the isle of Crete.
No man alive had greater pow'r or pelf,
by virtue of a first-rate merchant fleet
that scoured the seas in search of wealth.
One day, while musing on his luck,
the king was struck with gratitude
and hit upon an innovative trick
to solemnize this humble attitude.
He made a pledge to Lord Poseidon
to sacrifice the first thing to arise
from the depths—whatever rode the tide in.
A speck on the horizon met his gaze.
On close inspection, to be brief,
the speck turned out to be a bull;
not your ordinary side of beef,
but a very special breed of animal.
Its hide was white as a wedding gown
and soft as the tears of summer stars.
It tossed its head and pawed the ground,
wielding its horns like scimitars.

Minos felt it would be a waste
to slaughter such a precious specimen
and sacrificed another in its place,
keeping the bull to propagate its line.
The Lord of Waters was insulted
by the offer of a substitute
and a chain of incidents resulted
proving that gods cannot be duped.
Minos' wife conceived a passion
to mate with this majestic suitor
and commissioned Daedalus to fashion
a hollow cow so it could mount her.

The fruit of this unlikely union
was a monster called the Minotaur.
The bull ran rampant shortly after
its amorous encounter with the queen.
Each day revealed some new disaster,
another innocent bystander slain.
Eurystheus, bored with life at court,
perked up when told about the bull.
He hoped his rival might be gored
grappling with a beast that powerful.
Thus Heracles set sail for Crete.
Once there, he found the king absorbed
in some weighty affairs of state,
with strict orders not to be disturbed.
The strong man craved an audience
to ask for the king's assistance,
but when he finally gained admittance,
he was regarded with indifference.

The son of Zeus was irritated,
indignant at the king's rebuff.
Resolved to do the task unaided,
he exited the palace in a huff.
He found the bovine behemoth
roaming freely beside the sea.
It tossed its head as if to scoff
and pawed the sand repeatedly.
Quickly doffing his lion cape,
Alcides played the gallant matador.
He fluttered the enticing drape
the way an angler jiggles a lure.
After more than a dozen passes,
he began behaving recklessly.
The ease of previous successes
gave him a false sense of security.
The bull made an unexpected turn
and caught the hero from behind.
For a split second he was airborne
till his flying buttress hit the sand.

Quickly regaining composure,
he whirled to face his nemesis
just as the cud-chewing bulldozer
was about to deal the coup de grâce.
Vaulting with an almost feline jump,
Alcides somersaulted in mid-air,
inventing by this acrobatic stunt
a sport that later flourished there.[3]

The pair proceeded to engage
in a contest of sheer bone and muscle
so common in that brutal age
when even gods were prone to scuffle.
The bull was strong as oxen go,
but if it had ten times the strength
that ordinary, stall-fed cattle do,
it couldn't last for any length.
Exercising routine caution,
Alcides trounced the bull tout de suite,
which lay down, panting from exhaustion,
thus tacitly acknowledging defeat.
He crossed the saline sea to Greece,
riding astride its ample back
and managing the reins with ease,
for now the bull was tame and meek.
Eurystheus let the ox go free
but, lapsing into vicious habits,
it ran amok, killing haphazardly,
for bulls are your worst recidivists.
There was a rumor current then
about a king named Diomedes
who governed Thrace—a Scythian
who, despite lugubrious entreaties,
slew all unsuspecting strangers
and used their mutilated corpses
to stock a set of brazen mangers
where they were eaten by his horses.

Eurystheus ordered Heracles
to yoke the four man-eating mares
and drive them as a team to Greece
on crowded public thoroughfares.
Mustering a hasty levy
of young, two-fisted fighting men,
Alcides led his little navy
to Thrace. The ship outstripped the wind.
The crew docked at various ports,
their first stop being Thessaly,
hotbed of foul play, eldritch arts,
black sabbaths and necromancy.
Before proceeding with my tale,
I have to give a brief account
of prior events in some detail
whose significance is paramount.
One day, Apollo, feeling spunky,
spied a cute, curvaceous virgin
astride a gallant little donkey
that capered at her gentle urging.
The sight of such a sexy waif
riding bareback gave him the hots.
He wooed her with a godly gift:
some bonbons in a heart-shaped box.
He propositioned, she demurred.
He persisted, she resisted.
He made her laugh, she dropped her guard.
He waltzed off with her maidenhead.

Time passed like a narcotic dream.
The days flowed smoothly as a river.
The memory of the god grew dim
and the lass—Coronis—took a lover.
A crow, that interfering bird,
happened to see the pair in bed
and told Apollo what he'd heard,
the soft endearments that were said.

Apollo was a jealous god.
He burst into the lovers' room
and plunged a bodkin in her bod,
cutting the foetus from her womb.[4]
Repenting of this irrational act,
he captured the officious crow
and dyed it blacker than a bat,
which hitherto was white as snow.
Delivered by Caesarian section,
the child was cleped Asclepius
and entrusted to the Centaur Chiron
to cultivate his budding genius.
The Centaur taught him botany
and how to cauterize a wound.
He learned comparative anatomy
dissecting insects he had found.
Every single fact or facet
pertaining to the human body
took on a fascinating aspect
and became the boy's peculiar study.

By the time he reached maturity,
Asclepius was so deeply read
in arcane authors of antiquity,
it was quipped he could raise the dead.
When Theseus' son, Hippolytus,
who preferred wildlife to women
—a devotee of buskined Artemis—
fell victim to his step-mom's venom,
the goddess, to save her votary,
beseeched the eminent physician
to apply some sovereign remedy
and restore his former condition.
Asclepius treated the cadaver,
deftly flourishing his scalpel.
After much intensive labor,
a shallow pulse was palpable.
Hippolytus resumed the chase,
much to the goddess's delight,

but the implications of the case
troubled Zeus on his chilly height.
"If one man be allowed the chance
to abrogate the laws of nature,
the gods will lose preeminence
and our decrees will cease to matter."
Saying thus, the cloud-compeller
unpacked a box of thunderbolts,
but had to rummage in the cellar
to find one with sufficient volts.

Asclepius perished in a flash,
a warning to all innovators.
His body was reduced to ash
and strewn about by sportive zephyrs.
Phoebus, craving retribution
for such an unjust penalty,
avenged his son's electrocution
by traveling to sunny Sicily.
Beneath the crater of Mt. Aetna
that belched forth incandescent plumes
of smoke and streams of molten lava,
the Cyclopes toiled amid the fumes.
The volcano held the smithy
where Arges, Brontes and Steropes
forged the heavy artillery
Zeus hurled against his enemies.
As they assembled thunderbolts
to meet the quota set by Zeus,
Apollo snuck up on the dolts
and cut their throats in one fell swoop.
Zeus refused to brook such hubris.
For his insubordination,
Apollo was sold to King Admetus,
trading his harp in for an apron.
As he was tidying the kitchen,
the three Weird Sisters came a-calling.
Clotho, with thinly veiled derision
sighed: "Tsk-tsk, how the mighty have fallen!"

The toothless hags cackled with glee,
amused at their own raillery.
Apollo answered good-naturedly
and made them shriek with every repartee.
In time the conversation turned
to how the god was being treated.
Atropos said she was concerned,
a theme all three reiterated.
Apollo told them not to worry,
Admetus was a veritable saint,
the most beloved man in Pherae,
and gave him no grounds for complaint.
"Pity he has to die so young,"
Lachesis blurted inadvertently,
and Atropos snapped: "Mind your tongue!"
casting a spiteful glance her way.
"Wouldn't you ladies like some wine?"
Apollo offered, acting nonchalant.
"This old Falernian is really fine.
Come on, Admetus gives me all I want!"
The Sisters weren't at all averse
to taking an occasional nip.
In fact, good wine was far too scarce
to turn their crooked noses up.
At first, they took a drink for thirst.
It was so good, a second beckoned.
The third they sampled just for taste
till they were three sheets to the wind.

Amid the general hilarity,
Apollo managed to persuade
Death's debt collection agency
Admetus' fate should be delayed.
They agreed on a compromise:
Admetus' thread would not be cut
if, at the time of his demise,
he could produce a willing substitute.
Admetus, learning of the deal,
thought it would be an easy thing

to find some patriotic fool
who'd die for his beloved king.
But when he put it to the test,
his request was greeted with disdain,
for each one loves his own life best
and calls it blest, however mean.
"Surely my father or mother,"
he thought, "will die to save their son."
But neither would forsake the other
or leave their love to face the world alone.
The hour of doom was drawing near.
The king withdrew to an unlit room
and brooded in his favorite chair,
compounding the surrounding gloom.
As he sat immersed in this brown study,
glumly staring into empty space,
his wife, Alcestis, renowned for beauty
and every charm that gives a body grace,

touched his arm and said: "Admetus,
you overlooked the only person
who stood ready at a moment's notice
to forfeit life for your redemption."
These words, said with such conviction,
touched Admetus to the very core.
Till then he'd thought love just a fiction
invented by some drunken troubadour.
At first he wasn't sure whether
he wanted worse to cry or laugh:
to cry at losing such a treasure
or laugh at finding such a wife.
He gradually realized, however,
the more he pondered on his loss
that, despite our best endeavor,
love sometimes exacts an awful cost.
When Heracles took a brief hiatus
on his way to tame the Thracian mares
to pay a call on his friend Admetus,
he found the hall a scene of grief and tears.

After the usual courtesies,
observing his careworn demeanor,
Alcides asked his pal of former days
who all the funeral pomp was for.
Not wanting to upset his guest,
Admetus improvised a fib
that sharper marksmen would have missed,
for he was a dab hand at ad lib.

"A humble woman," he intoned,
"who served my family well for years
and loved our children as her own,
has gone to meet her ancestors."
"Your sentiments are very noble,"
said Heracles, "but somewhat misplaced.
You shouldn't go to so much trouble
for a slave. They're easily replaced."
Once settled in the guest quarters,
Alcides pulled out all the stops,
calling for wine, barking orders,
and shouting ribald songs over his cups.
One of Admetus' old retainers,
a major-domo proud of his station,
resenting Heracles' ill manners,
couldn't contain his indignation.
"The queen is barely in her grave
and all you care about is drinking!
Is that the way true friends behave?"
He paused to let his words sink in.
The son of Zeus sat bolt upright.
"The queen? I thought it was a slave!"
It was as if a miniature light
blinked on inside a mammoth cave.
Grabbing the old man by the collar,
he demanded: "Where's Alcestis' tomb?"
He answered in a raspy whisper:
"Near the cave called the Witch's Womb!"

Heracles hastened to the spot
where earlier that afternoon
Alcestis' coffin had been brought,
for Death was due to meet her soon.
Coming to a densely wooded dell,
the hero saw a hooded figure
he recognized as Death himself
stalking toward Alcestis' sepulchre.
They reached the tomb simultaneously
where Alcestis lay like a stone gisant.
Alcides blocked the marble passageway,
preventing Death from entering the vault.
The skull and crossbones you can see
on many harsh and toxic solvents,
does not do justice to, much less convey
a faithful image of, Death's lineaments.
O Muse, who ever guides my pen,
grant me the talent to describe
Death's features to dull-witted men
and earn the plaudits of my tribe.
Death has a slow and measured gait.
Aside from this peculiar feature,
he demonstrates no telltale trait
and seems a man of average stature.
But Death's outstanding attribute
is his air of supreme authority.
No emperor could be more absolute,
or Pope residing in his Holy See.

Those who quietly accept their fate,
he leads in easy stages down to Hell.
Those who struggle and vociferate,
he drags by force, kick how they will.
In his most condescending voice,
Death asked: "Do you know who I am?"
The son of Zeus replied: "Oh yes,
I know. I just don't give a damn."

Incensed at this insubordination,
King Mort resorted to violence,
but when he tried to force his way in,
he met with formidable resistance.
In the ensuing altercation,
Death found himself so sore bestead
that, forgetful of his reputation,
he trusted to his heels and fled.
Returning later that evening
with one dressed like a mendicant,
Heracles found the king still grieving.
The florid hall was richly redolent.
Admetus welcomed his return
and asked the hero where he'd been,
for he was curious to learn
the mystery of his hooded friend.
The stranger bore a strong resemblance
to someone he'd often seen before,
and brought poor Alcestis to remembrance
—but that was utter madness, to be sure.

Now it was Heracles' turn to stretch
the truth and pull the wool over his eyes.
He said he'd won her at a wrestling match
at which she constituted the first prize,
and he asked Admetus if he'd watch
the girl till he returned from overseas.
Admetus was at first reluctant,
too grief-stricken to even touch her,
but Heracles was adamant,
insisting he would trust no other.
His arguments at length prevailed.
Admetus took her tender hand in his,
and when the hooded maiden was unveiled,
who should stand revealed but Alcestis.

.

Book VIII

Over the course of milleniums
with their recurrent pageantry,
there have arisen certain customs
revered for their great antiquity.
The rationale behind such rules
is often garbled in transmission,
leading some rash, misguided fools
to dismiss them as mere superstition.
Look at what took place in Britain!
Some cows were given meat to eat
instead of hay. They went insane,
as did those who ate the tainted beef.
When people carelessly ignore
the old, time-honored practices
and precepts coined in days of yore,
they reap the bitter consequences.
Making his way back to the coast,
Heracles rejoined his forces,
still mindful of Eurystheus' behest
to tame the four man-eating horses.
The mares belonged to Diomedes,
a sordid man with brutal tendencies
who lorded it over the Bistones,
a northern race of warlike savages.

There was a sacred obligation
back then to take wayfarers in.
Strangers needing food and lodging
fell under the gods' protection.
Diomedes, it will be remembered,
would slay his houseguests unawares.
Their lifeless bodies were dismembered
and fed to his carnivorous mares.
Heracles and his hand-picked band
of toughs made land near Tirida.

Telling his men to wait behind,
he struck out toward the interior.
Proceeding inland several miles,
the son of Zeus began to notice
large piles of bones at intervals,
relics of Diomedes' slaughterhouse.
He arrived just after nightfall
at what seemed a peaceful village.
Not far off, he heard the primal
muzhik of wild dogs bent on pillage.
It wasn't hard to recognize
the Mongol mogul's domicile,
conspicuous among those hovels as
the Taj Mahal in Hooterville.
The stables formed a separate wing,
with living quarters for the grooms
who, done with their mundane routine,
were getting pickled in their rooms.

Inside the labyrinthine stable
—dark, crowded, stifling, slick with dung—
he worked as fast as he was able
to ferret out the fearsome foursome.
The horses sported iron chains
because of their high-protein diet,
which must have warped their equine brains,
for they were quick to kick and bite.
Hitching the quartet together,
he led them off the property,
but the chains' succinct craquelure
alerted the grooms to the robbery.
Hindered by his ungainly freight,
the son of Zeus had little choice
but to await the thugs and fight,
for eight of them had given chase.
Las Vegas odds were eight to one,
but smart money favored Heracles.
He pummeled them as they came on
and made a bundle for the bookies.

With the front-runners out of the race,
he spurred the rabid circus ponies
back to his waiting crew posthaste,
pursued by a swarm of mad Bistones.
Next morning, as disheveled Dawn
had just begun to yawn and stretch,
unwilling to resign the eiderdown
of fleecy clouds and fluffy coverlets,

the hero reached some rising ground
in view of camp. Waving his sword,
he signaled from atop the mound
to warn his men of the approaching horde.
Abderus, the Achaean chieftain's
aide-de-camp ran to meet him there.
Heracles handed him the reins
and turned to the business of war.
The enemy van was disorganized,
advancing with no coherent plan.
The veteran Greeks capitalized
on the Thracians' lack of discipline.
Sparing neither horse nor rider,
they slaughtered so efficiently,
it might have looked to an outsider
like some group seppuku ceremony.
From amid the fray, Alcides spied
Diomedes charging through the ranks
in his chariot, swerving side to side
to rally his badly shattered flanks.
Using his sword to cut a swath,
he plotted his trajectory
to intersect the warlord's path
and interdict his bid for victory.
Careening through the rank and file,
the tyrant struck an obstacle.
Heracles clocked him Ty Cobb-style
with his club—a line drive to the skull.

When Diomedes plunged headfirst
and lay immobile on the plain,
a rumor spread throughout the host
the sadistic ruler had been slain.
The ragtag regiment dispersed,
checkmated by the Greek platoon.
While this revue was being staged
with bows and curtain calls for all,
a Grand Guignol was underway
with Abderus cast in the lead rôle.
The youth was strong and capable,
and very shrewd for one his age,
but the mares were rudely powerful
and proved too mutinous to manage.
The horses bolted down the hill
the moment they were left alone.
Like mussels clinging to the hull
of a ship or a dog clenching a bone,
the faithful squire held on until
his skull was shattered on a stone.
By the time Heracles reached the scene
with Diomedes' flaccid bulk in tow,
the mares had scoured Abderus' skeleton
clean, which greatly upset the crew.
Their appetite not fully sated
—for Abderus was a mere hors d'oeuvre—
the mares were sumptuously fêted
on Diomedes, just as he deserved.

Heracles built Abderus a tomb
and buried his remains with dignity.
The site was colonized by some
of his cohorts and became a city.[5]
Their hunger having been allayed,
the mares submitted to the bit
and carried Heracles with speed
to Greece in Diomedes' chariot.
Eurystheus lost all his nerve
on seeing the nags and froze in terror,

but summoning a small reserve
of guts, he devoted them to Hera.
They were let loose to range at will
on Mt. Olympus, where they strayed,
cropping green grass until they fell
afoul of predators and were destroyed.
Their offspring survived, however,
till the Greeks took Helen back from Paris,
or that later champion, Alexander,[6]
conquered the world astride Bucephalus.
Eurystheus had an only daughter
whose face could sink the Seventh Fleet.
Admete couldn't catch a suitor.
In fact, she couldn't even get a date.
Hearing one day of Ares' girdle,
a garment from Hephaestus' textile mill
that made the wearer irresistible,
Admete begged her father for the frill.

The girdle graced the slender hips
of Queen Hippolyta, the Amazon
who led the dreaded tribe of feminists
encamped along the river Thermodon.
Eurystheus was a doting father
and saw a chance to finish Heracles;
ergo, to pacify his daughter,
he sent the hero to fetch the prize.
The Amazons were matriarchal,
i.e. ruled exclusively by women.
Their customs were unnatural,
ranging to the cruel and inhuman.
They crippled all their male children
to keep them in abject subjection.
A man's place was in the kitchen
serving his mistress' every whim.
The right breast of every young girl
was cut off so as not to interfere
when they shot a bow or went to hurl
the light and accurate Amazon spear.

Assembling yet another crew,
including such men of proven worth
as Iolaus, his favorite nephew,
Peleus, whose goddess wife gave birth
to Achilles, the fierce Myrmidon
remembered chiefly for his wrath,
Peleus' brother, brave Telamon,
father of the redoubtable Ajax,

who helped topple Troy, Theseus,
who slew the loathsome Minotaur
and fought beside King Pirithous
against the Centaurs, and many more,
Heracles, in a single ship,
set sail with this troupe of heroes.
Making an impromptu pit stop
for fresh water at the isle of Paros,
he sent ashore two lesser lights
with jars, who were routinely slain,
for Minos' sons had mineral rights
and closely guarded their domain.
Swiftly assessing the situation,
Alcides took decisive action,
killing them without compunction
for their gratuitous aggression.
Not satisfied by this quid pro quo
—for his crew was nonetheless reduced—
Heracles harassed the Parians so,
they offered him his pick of substitutes.
He chose none other than Alcaeus,
their king, and his brother Sthenelus,
offspring of Minos' son, Androgeus,
to take the murdered sailors' place.
Clearing the Hellespont and Bosphorus,
they sailed into the Axine Sea,
which Heracles renamed Euxeinus[7]
in token of its calm and clemency.

Mariandyne lay along the route

and here the heroes stopped to rest.
King Lycus knew them by repute
and threw the crew a lavish feast.
Proceeding to Themiscyra,
they put a dime in the parking meter
and waited for Queen Hippolyta,
who made the scene a short time later.
Hippolyta was, let's say—way hip,
a lean, mean queen; a sailor's dream.
The dominatrix boarded ship,
her booty glowing like a golden flame.
The heroes parted as she passed,
forming a human corridor,
and every wagging tongue was hushed
to watch the dusky woman warrior.
At last, her searching gaze alighted
on Heracles, who just sat passive
in the stern. She grinned, delighted
by his physique, so hard and massive.
Rightly inferring him to be
the leader of the expedition,
she asked Alcides candidly
the thrust or purpose of his mission.
"I'm on a delicate assignment,"
he said, choosing his words with care.
"I've come to get the golden garment
that guards your royal derrière."

She said: "I'm not a slave to fashion.
The girdle's yours on one condition.
First, you must satisfy my passion.
Then take it, you have my permission."
But their coitus was interruptus
before foreplay had even begun,
for Hera, as always, was jealous
lest the prize be too easily won.
Disguised in Amazon apparel,
the goddess spread a false report
Hippolyta was in dire peril,

kidnapped by foreigners in port.
Screaming like a female chorus
sight-reading Orff's Carmina Burana
before an amateur performance,
the Amazons attacked the harbor.
Suspecting the queen of treason,
Heracles forgot all about sex
and, needing no further reason,
smote the vixen with her own ax.
Then, disregarding decency,
he stripped the girdle from her corse
and tossed her body in the sea
without a morsel of remorse.
Riding bareback, the Amazons bore
the emblematic crescent shield
and other implements of war
that made them fearsome in the field.
What clothes they wore were made of fur
and the hides of animals they'd killed.

The melee started in the bay.
Alcides and his mercenaries
were dominant in the affray,
demolishing their adversaries.
Having beaten the brazen dames,
the victors paid another call
on Lycus, who was holding games
in honor of his brother's funeral.
Forgetting for the nonce their lust
for blood and loot, the crew had fun
competing in the heat and dust
like children romping in the sun.
When Lycus asked for volunteers
to match their skill as pugilists,
Titias, who surpassed his peers
in looks and strength, entered the lists.
He was the reigning champion
and the idol of the local girls,
with washboard abs, buns of iron,

and teeth like rows of cultured pearls.
The Greeks turned to the son of Zeus
reflexively as their best candidate.
It would have seemed cowardice to refuse,
so he took up the proffered gauntlet.
Prizes were to be awarded
and Lycus showed what these would be:
to the winner, a gold-embroidered
cloak; to the loser, a keg of brandy.

Divesting themselves of excess clothes
that might detract from their performance
and donning padded leather gloves,
the boxers adopted a fighting stance.
When Lycus gave the go-ahead,
the crowd erupted in a roar
as if a cloud broke overhead,
emitting a thunderous downpour.
Like a tribe of Huns or Vandals
assailing some impregnable height
or laying siege to castle walls,
Titias probed this way and that.
Both men warmed to the encounter,
engaging in some brief exchanges
that made the crowd wax even louder,
giving vent to oaths and expletives.
Then, like a moth circling a flame
that singes its delicate membranes,
Titias, lured by desire of acclaim,
paid the cost such hunger often claims.
Heracles threw a one-two punch.
The first blow dashed out all his teeth.
The second landed with a crunch,
ending the match in sudden death.
Let others praise the character
of saints like Francis of Assisi.
Although his morals weren't as pure,
Heracles was never called a sissy.

In proof of his profound regret
at causing poor Titias' demise,
Alcides fought a border war to get
back stolen land from Lycus' enemies.

Book IX

Each time a little sparrow falls,
we're told that God takes special note,
and every time a lost child calls,
God hears and hastens to the spot.
But such talk is utter nonsense,
for every day we see men thrive
who haven't got an ounce of conscience,
while those who do barely survive.
Don't prate about the law of karma
or praise Gautama when he avers
patience is the strongest armor.
He who waits and prays for justice, errs.
The casus belli is still unknown,
but the Olympians were in league.
Zeus was evicted from the throne,
a hapless victim of palace intrigue.
Employing adamantine fetters,
the rebel gods imprisoned Jove,
forging his signature on letters
till time should sanctify the move.
Zeus, at one time, was a suitor
of a lovely Nereid named Thetis.
In fact, he diligently wooed her
till warned to cool it by Prometheus.

Thetis, to save her former beau,
joined forces with Briareus,
who had a hundred hands or so,
making him armed and dangerous.
Together they foiled the cabal
and freed Zeus from captivity,
who laid a fine on every rebel,
thus reasserting his supremacy.
The gods Apollo and Poseidon
were forced to enter the employ
of a scoundrel named Laomedon
who ruled the windswept plains of Troy.

Poseidon worked as stonemason
while Apollo mixed the mortar.
In one short circuit of the sun,
the city walls were built to order.
Their term of service at an end,
the gods were eager to be paid,
for even gods need cash to spend
to bribe a judge or corrupt a maid.
Laomedon just laughed at their request.
"Pay you! Tell me, what have you done?
Do you call that work? Surely you jest!
Who supplied the tools and all the stone?"
To add insult to injury,
he said he'd tie them hand and foot
and sell them into slavery
unless they took the next ship out.

Then, feeling rather inventive,
he added as an afterthought
to give them further incentive,
he'd amputate their ears to boot.
Smarting beneath such obloquy,
the gods departed Troy at once.
On the way they held a colloquy
to formulate a suitable response.
Apollo sent a dreadful plague
to afflict the city's residents,
although historians are vague
as to the nature of this pestilence.
The texts are clearer with regard
to the harsh measures undertaken
by Poseidon, who sent Troy-ward
a fearsome sea serpent or kraken.
Like in some cheap sci-fi thriller,
it murdered people with abandon,
having studied acting with Godzilla,
who taught the ropes to keep his hand in.
Severely tried by plague and monster,
the Trojans prayed for some relief

and approached Laomedon in conster-
nation as their nation's acting chief.
Like any conscientious leader,
he went to consult an oracle,
which was the usual procedure
in times of political upheaval.

The oracles were managed by
Apollo and his sacred college,
a holy order like Freemasonry
that profited from bogus knowledge.
In answer to the question posed,
the priestess gave a brief riposte:
his own daughter must be exposed,
a morsel for the monster's repast.
Although a liar and a crook,
and no stranger to depravity,
the words Apollo's priestess spoke
took him aback, such was their gravity.
A man whose vices are apparent,
a scheming mind and vulgar tongue,
can likewise be a caring parent.
Even vipers cherish their own young.
The ruler thought: "It's only fair,
before I sacrifice my daughter,
the riffraff ought to donate their
brats to feed that blasted critter."
Laomedon returned to Troy,
where he was greeted with affection,
for people thought he'd learned a ploy
to rid them of their twin affliction.
When he told them what his plans were,
i.e. to feed their daughters to the beast,
they didn't care much for his answer.
His method didn't please them in the least.

There was a sudden exodus
of eligible young Trojan lasses.

Their parents made up some excuse
to bundle them to far-off places.
Phoenodamas had bucked the trend,
a widower endowed by luck with guts.
He kept his three girls home to tend
the hearth and mend his fishing nets.
Hiding behind the tawdry splendor
of office and the sanctity of laws,
Laomedon urged him to surrender
one of his daughters for the common cause.
Phoenodamas wasn't one of those
you could easily impose upon.
He knew a fish-head from a rose
and got a good whiff of Laomedon.
Speaking before a disgruntled throng,
he launched into a diatribe,
denouncing the leader loud and long
for the troubles dogging the Dardan tribe.
The crowd unnerved the Trojan Diet.
The elders, bowing to pressure,
in order to avert a riot,
made a conciliatory gesture.
The king agreed, on their advice,
in compliance with existing laws,
that the matter of the sacrifice
should be resolved by drawing straws.

Bigwig and fisherman both drew.
Call it blind chance or destiny,
the king's was the shorter of the two,
which meant the ax fell on Hesione.
Weeping and wailing piteously,
pleading and tearing at her locks,
she was taken, naked, to the sea,
where she was shackled to the rocks.
Hummingbirds and honeybees,
bred on nature's virgin nectar,
would spurn lush meadows just to gaze
at this kinswoman of mighty Hector.

Alcides, sailing back from where
the Amazons and he had clashed,
beheld the maiden shackled there
without a stitch, plainly abashed.
With every nerve on the alert
for action, they traversed the bay
and eased the vessel into port,
berthing her alongside the quay.
It wasn't hard to learn the truth;
the town was buzzing with the news.
Opinions ran from mouth to mouth,
expressing wildly divergent views.
It didn't take a British sleuth
to connect the relevant clues.
True to his noble avocation,
Heracles tracked Laomedon down
and offered, for a piece of the action,
to whack the monster for the Don.

In the old days, times were nasty.
The gods, embroiled in petty quarrels,
consoled themselves with pederasty
till Moses spoiled their fun with morals.
Zeus, cross-dressing as an eagle,
happened to be cruising over Troy,
pursuing some coy little she-gull,
when he observed a boffo shepherd boy.
Ganymede was the son of Tros
—the king from whom Troy took its name—
Laomedon's grandfather, source
of bearded Homer's far-flung fame.
Swooping down on ponderous pinions,
Zeus zeroed in on Ganymede,
seizing him in his avid talons
as sheep stood bleating in the mead.
He took the prepossessing mite
back to his Olympian haunts,
where the lad became his catamite,
tending to his domestic wants.

As for Tros, he was so morose
over the disappearance of his son
that his prayers miraculously rose
to the casements of Zeus' mansion.
To show he was a regal eagle
(the boy had proved so amiable
and kidnapping was still illegal)
Zeus found his grief regrettable.

To recompense his fervent prayers
and render his loss less painful,
Zeus gave the king a brace of mares,
immortal steeds from his own stable.
These nags were poetry in motion.
They could run atop standing wheat
or skim the surface of the ocean
without so much as wetting their feet.
The wondrous plugs were handed on
when Tros died to his epigones;
first to Ilus, then Laomedon,
when he interred his father's bones.
When Heracles, to slay the kraken,
asked for the mares as his reward,
the two men struck a hasty bargain,
relying solely on each other's word.
Sea monsters normally feed on fish,
content with such a plentiful diet,
but once they've tasted human flesh,
it's hard to break them of the habit.
Leaving Hesione chained as bait,
Heracles and his crew erected
a wall that rose to a strategic height
so the ingénue would be protected.
Wide as is the gap that separates
gods from heroes, heroes from mere men,
or ordinary men from gifted apes,
reptiles fall still lower on the chain.

Its instincts honed to crude perfection
through eons of relentless strife,
where every failure spelled extinction
and ruthless cunning held the key to life,
the serpent slurped ashore near Troy.
Its nostrils spewed out jets of spray
as it approached the dainty decoy,
scenting the telltale odor of fresh prey.
Upon encountering the wall,
the snake, not easy to deter,
proceeded to mount the obstacle,
poking its snout beyond the barrier.
To give a rough approximation
of the size of this prodigious dragon,
it could, without exaggeration,
have swallowed an entire Volkswagen.
When it saw Hesione with all
her tender flesh exposed to view,
it unhinged its dehiscent maw,
leaving no doubt what it meant to do.
Heracles, equipped for battle,
burst from concealment in a flash
and ran for the gap full throttle,
leaping into the creature's crevasse.
Stunned for an instant, the serpent
had no other choice but to swallow.
The onlookers lining the battlement
remarked: "That was one loco gringo!"

The kraken, having snagged a snack
and dined on hero à la mode,
retired inside an old shipwreck
that mouldered on the ocean's bed.
There, within the rotting timber
of some sunken vessel's cargo hold,
a ship once made of finest lumber
that carried spices, silk and gold,
Alcides struggled with his fear,
recalling all the prophecies

that gave him strength to persevere
in the face of grave uncertainties.
Three days he waited in the womb
of death, sealed like a chrysalis,
entombed in this disgusting catacomb,
three nights in this sarcophagus.
Clutching his dagger's reassuring heft,
he plunged it in the monster's viscera,
cutting till there was nothing left
but what lawyers call disjecta membra.
Having dissected the giant snake,
Alcides used his trenchant blade
to safely effect his own escape,
slitting a passage in its side.
The townsfolk gave him up for lost,
so when he showed up looking hale,
a few old biddies said he was a ghost.
At any rate, it made a pretty tale.

His first task on coming ashore
was to remove Hesione's shackles.
He found her, naked as before,
and loosed the galling manacles.
Now that the cruel ordeal was o'er,
Hesione soughed a thousand sighs.
He spoke kind words to comfort her
and gently wiped her weeping eyes.
Alcides noticed something odd
and raised a hand to scratch his poll.
The monster's stomach acid had
left him bald as a bowling ball.
That night was capped by revelry.
His naked pate was food for laughter
among his crew, whose raillery
he parried with good-humored banter.
Next morning, a Trojan embassy
arrived leading a team of horses.
The envoys swore by Charon's ferry
these were Zeus' own immortal coursers.

"I'm sure they run like quicksilver,"
the hero said, not lightly taken in
by every shameless, two-bit huckster.
"All the same, I'll take them for a spin."
As if to cut short all debate,
he straddled a steed at random
and took off like a scalded cat,
leading the other mare in tandem.

Not wishing to prolong the matter,
he spurred the bangtails toward the bay
and rode out in the glaucous water,
where they sank to his profound dismay.
Returning with the soggy mares,
Alcides chided the emissaries
for trafficking in shoddy wares,
berating them for their perjuries.
"And tell your king, Laomedon,"
he said, "he'll sing a different tune
when I come back to sack this town
and level every faithless stone."
He passed the word to weigh anchor
and trained his gaze on the horizon.
For now he'd have to waive his anger
till time allowed his plans to ripen.
Voyaging home by way of Thrace,
the heroes paid a call on Poltys,
who entertained them for a space
and showered them with farewell gifts.
As they were pulling out of port,
Alcides shot and killed Sarpedon.
He was Poltys' brother, and the sort
who makes this weary life a burden.
Touching at the isle of Thasos,
he subjugated the inhabitants
and gave it to the pair from Paros
to rule, i.e. King Minos' descendants.

At Torone, the son of Zeus
was challenged to a wrestling match
by Polygonus and Telegonus,[8]
whom he disposed of with despatch.
When Heracles arrived in Hellas,
he relayed the golden panties
to Eurystheus whence, alas,
they languished on Admete's nates.

Book X

When man was in his infancy,
a babe unable to discern
hard facts from childish fantasy
and had the IQ of a fern,
his voice was inarticulate
and uttered uncouth groans and grunts.
With these he could communicate
only his most fundamental wants.
As he continued to progress,
his language played a crucial rôle
in mankind's overall success.
He found it was a useful tool.
The invention of an alphabet
was an important innovation.
The slender reed and clay tablet
paved the way for civilization.
Enter the unassuming bard,
scald or scop, call him what you will,
who earned a meager livelihood
by means of his linguistic skill.
If it weren't for the poet's work
to make our language flow with ease,
we'd still be grubbing in the dirt
or swinging naked from the trees.

Off the coast of Iberia,
which nowadays is known as Spain,
an island called Erytheia
lay anchored in the restless main.
On the island stood a castle,
imparting a grandeur to the scene
of stunted trees and russet cattle,
like a picture from a magazine.
In the castle lived Spain's sovereign,
the triple-bodied giant Geryon,
who had the strength of twenty oxen
and dined on vinegar and carrion.

When Eurystheus learned of Geryon,
he thought: "This time his ass is mine!"
and ordered the son of Amphitryon
to retrieve the ornery giant's kine.
Ancient Europe was rife with dangers,
a virgin wild, pristine and feral,
where wolves would waylay wayfarers,
who traveled at their own peril.
To make the highway safe for pilgrims
and rid the countryside of vermin,
Alcides slew a slew of Isengrims[9]
and other of their cousins-german.
At the southern tip of Iberia,
he surveyed the narrow isthmus
connecting Spain with Africa,
a tactically important nexus.

Whether to display his muscle,
or maybe to discourage war,
or else facilitate sea travel
—whatever his true reasons were—
he thrust the continents asunder
as far as his two arms could reach.
They parted with a muffled thunder.
Time and tide widened the breach.
Now the daystar, waxing hotter,
turned all the air to liquid fire.
That and lack of drinking water
combined to rouse the hero's ire.
He notched an arrow on the gut
and sent it singing toward the sun.
Though it fell short of the target,
it caused the Titan some concern.
Helios shouted: "Jehoshaphat!
Have you forgotten who I am?
I thought I was hot-headed but
you mortals put us gods to shame!"
Heracles was dutifully contrite.
The sun admired his rude vitality

and eased back on his thermostat,
not one to be outshone in courtesy.
King Sol, in a magnanimous
gesture, loaned Heracles his yacht
to cross the aqueous impasse,
a kind of golden chamber pot.

He launched out on the open main,
but Oceanus, to test his mettle,
unleashed a fiendish hurricane
that threatened to upset the kettle.
Once more Alcides drew his bow,
aimed this time at Oceanus' breast.
His arrow scared the old salt so,
the Titan squelched the tempest-blast.
Arriving at his rendezvous,
he climbed a nearby elevation
to get a panoramic view
and scan his field of operation.
Geryon's cattle were guarded
by the herdsman Eurytion
and Orthrus, his dual-headed
watchdog and stalwart companion.
The canny canine spotted him
as Heracles crouched on the hill
and ran to tear him limb from limb,
its black lips drawn back in a snarl.
When Orthrus came in striking distance,
Heracles bludgeoned both its heads.
The herdsman rushed to its assistance
and joined his pet among the shades.
The son of Zeus was rounding up
the cattle scattered hither and yon
and loading them aboard the cup
when he was confronted by Geryon.

The giant was widely thought to be
the strongest man in existence.

Fact is, he wasn't one but three,
like immense Siamese triplets.
Add to his gargantuan stature
an attitude like Genghis Khan,
you had a formula for disaster,
like three Attilas in a single Hun.
Geryon mocked his opponent,
advising him to surrender.
Heracles answered the bonehead
with an arrow—a poignant rejoinder.
The guided missile did its job.
It entered through the giant's side
and skewered him like shish kebab.
He pirouetted awkwardly and died.
Gathering the remaining cows,
Alcides crossed the sea again,
returning the goblet to Helios
once he regained the coast of Spain.
He drove the herd through Roncevaux,
where Roland's rearguard bore the brunt
of an attack by the unbaptized foe,
while Ganelon rode comfortably in front.
Near the city of Massilia,
where the Rhône river disembogues,
began the province of Liguria,
ruled over by a pair of rogues.

Ialebion and Dercynus
grew up in grinding poverty
and early overcame their shyness
of committing highway robbery.
Plodding along the coast of France,
the shambling cattle raised a cloud.
Alcides used a leafy branch
to prod them on, exhorting them aloud.
The bandits, as was their custom,
assembled a devoted coterie
to overawe their chosen victim
and reinforce their outlawry.

Expecting little opposition
from one so visibly outnumbered,
they issued an ultimatum,
but this was no average cowherd.
The son of Zeus let loose a flight
of feathered messengers. Not birds
endowed with human speech. In fight,
a bow is far more eloquent than words.
The brothers were the first to fall.
The others scurried like a pack
of wharf rats scrambling from the hull
of some frigate ruptured on a rock.
The remnant rallied to the phrase:
"Worth stealing is worth fighting for!"
and gave themselves to this emprise
with all the ardor of a holy war.

The outcome was still undecided
when Heracles ran out of arrows
and knelt down, wounded and exhausted,
but Zeus took pity on his sorrows.
In a show of paternal love,
Zeus blew a storm cloud to the scene
whose gravid womb released a trove
of granite hailstones on the plain.
Replenished with ammunition,
Alcides shelled them with such chaleur,
the beleaguered bandits chose discretion
as the less repugnant part of valor.
Though he triumphed in the battle,
the hero's woes were far from over.
He still had miles to drive the cattle,
vast tracts of rough terrain to cover.
Crossing the Alps, the Matterhorn,
whose matter warps the woof of space,
loomed like some Brobdingnagian Norn
rehearsing Ragnarok in runic verse.
Before they reached the other side,
Alcides had to kick the asses

of robber bands who made a trade
of taxing traffic through the passes.
Leaving behind the Apennines,
they passed through groves of olive trees
and terraced hillsides thick with vines
where Italy unfurls its tapestries.

Arriving at the Tiber river,
at that time called the Albula,
Heracles met King Evander,
an outcast from Arcadia.
Ostracized as a parricide,
he and his followers left home
and colonized the riverside
on the future site of ancient Rome.
The exiled king invited him
to put his feet up for awhile
and catered to his every whim
with lavish hand—fish, flesh and fowl.
The chieftains traded anecdotes,
glad to be in kindred company.
The wine flowed freely and the liquid notes
of flute girls fanned their bonhomie.
Heracles, having drunk and feasted,
took leave of his newfound ally,
relieving those he'd entrusted
with the herd while he was on congé.
He drove the cows across the river
where there was foliage to browse
and lay down on a patch of verdure,
drowsy from all the food and booze.
Nearby, in a forest cavern,
lived a fierce, fire-breathing shepherd,
innkeeper of a grisly tavern
none ever left once having entered.

Kakos was a repulsive ghoul
with disturbing tastes—a cannibal.

No bones about it, he was cruel,
a connoisseur of man and animal.
Perceiving Heracles was blotto,
he seized four heifers by the tail
and dragged them backward to his grotto,
the better to disguise his trail.
When morning came, the sun's levee
wakened Heracles with its heat.
Still groggy from his drunken spree,
he struggled clumsily to his feet.
Before he drove the cattle on,
the hero counted every one
and, noticing a few were gone,
he set about to track them down.
He trailed the cows to Kakos' den,
but all their tracks led out, not in.
The entrance to the cave had been
sealed off with a humongous stone.
Alcides scratched his crown in wonder,
bewildered by the caveman's guile.
The cretin grinned behind the boulder.
The thought of fresh meat made him drool.
All creatures share an affinity
or sympathy with their own kind
and are joined by consanguinity
in a mutual concinnity of mind.

As Heracles prepared to leave,
some of the cows began to low,
to which the cattle in the cave
responded with a plaintive moo.
This echo was a catalyst
that triggered anagnorisis,
which is when the protagonist
faces facts and acts on the crisis.
Realizing he'd been cozened,
Alcides tossed aside the boulder,
a weight that would have made a dozen
sumo wrestlers wet their diaper.

The sun god's purifying rays
were loath to enter such a place.
The stench emitted by the cave
made solfatara seem like frankincense.
Kakos belched flames as vehement
as if he'd drunk a quart of Sterno,
but the hero's cape was fire-resistant
and he boldly stormed the inferno.
He cuffed Kakos like a mottled pup
and slued him like a screwball boomerang;
in short, he beat him to a pulp,
the way a French chef treats meringue.
To show his father proper thanks,
Heracles built Zeus an altar
of turf along the Tiber's banks,
assisted by his friend Evander.

He slaughtered one of the recovered
cows as a pious sacrifice.
Alcides' genius was revered
thereafter with religious rites.
Continuing his cavalcade
through southern Italy's campagna,
he came upon a tranquil glade
and kicked back for a quick siesta.
The relentless stridulation
of cicadas in succession rose
and faded like an air-raid siren,
disrupting Heracles' repose.
"Damn those blasted bugs to Hades!"
he growled, and the attendant gods
took heed. Since then, no more cicadas
have bombinated in those woods.
While Heracles was copping zees,
a bull broke away from its mates
and, absconding into choppy seas,
swam to Sicily across the straits.
The son of Zeus, upon perceiving
one of the bulls had gone awol

and seeing its hoofprints leading
to the sea, took the plunge as well.
He had to steer clear of the channel
that harbored Scylla's vicious pups
and Charybdis' all-consuming funnel,
whose vortex swallowed passing ships.

Once on shore, he didn't dawdle.
He tracked the bull to an estate
and found it mingled with the cattle
belonging to a petty potentate.
Eryx was a vain and haughty king,
offspring of mighty Aphrodite.
The naughty goddess had a fling
with Butes, Eryx' wastrel daddy.
The king, unwilling to resign
so fine a prize, proposed a bet:
his crown against Alcides' kine,
to the victor in a wrestling bout.
Alcides' whole life had been geared
to overcome hardship and danger.
It's no wonder then he little feared
this well-fed devotee of pleasure.
Repairing to the palaestra,
the wrestlers girded up their loins,
divesting themselves of extra
clothes, except what modesty enjoins.
Eryx was a dexterous wrestler.
His pampered body gleamed with oil,
anointed by his private trainer.
Heracles applied his own meanwhile.
No sooner had the gong been rung
than Eryx charged into the ring,
cocksure of victory. He was wrong,
and this mistake was his undoing.

The king discovered early on
Alcides was no neophyte.

Grappling with the man of iron
was like trying to drown a trout.
Perhaps if he were given time
to reconsider his rash wager,
the tyrant might have been inclined
to make amends for past behavior.
We'll never know. With quick precision,
Alcides clean and jerked the jerk
and held him briefly in suspension
before dashing his body in the dirt.
Entrusting to the hoi polloi
the guidance of the ship of state
till one of his own progeny
could claim it at a later date,
Alcides crossed the strait again,
towed this time by the vagrant bull.
They rejoined the herd, which by then
had wandered to a neighboring vale.
Proceeding up the eastern coast,
they left the land of Italy,
the home of Caesar and the Pope,
of Virgil, Dante and da Vinci.
Rounding the Adriatic Sea,
Hellas loomed up ahead and yet,
the son of Zeus was not home free.
The goddess Hera saw to that.

She sent a gadfly to harass
the cows with its sadistic bite.
Her gambit was a stunning success:
the cattle scattered far and wide.
It took all Heracles could do
to re-collect the straying herd,
and even then he missed a few,
but he was tired of all that merde.
He drove the wide-browed cattle home
to Tiryns where pious Eurystheus
burnt them in a splendid hecatomb
to cow-eyed Hera, divine protectress.

Book XI

Though myths may seem illogical,
a cross between a cock and bull,
more often they're paradoxical,
a pearl of wisdom in an oyster shell.
Heracles had, in eight years' time,
successfully performed all ten
of the tasks Eurystheus assigned,
so technically his job was done.
But the king, that exalted drone,
rejected labors two and five
because his nephew helped with one
and he'd done the other for a tithe.
His only hope for a future
without Nemesis dogging his heels
was for Heracles to endure
two more arbitrary ordeals.
Though it taxed his ingenuity,
Eurystheus conceived a scheme
so perverse in its absurdity
as to be brutal in the extreme.
Where the effulgent sun disk sets
after its final heat has been run,
at the ne plus ultra of the west,
of dubious existence, dimly known,

there blossomed a prolific garden,
home to many a pollen-crusted bee,
a green riot, rank with vegetation,
most notably a golden apple tree.
It was an apple from this tree
that lost the race for Atalanta
and sicced the dogs of war on Troy,
things never said of a banana.
Atlas was the garden's warden,
and it was he who built the wall
that girded it and set a dragon
to be its hundred-headed sentinel.

"Find the legendary garden."
The king unveiled his masterstroke.
"Overcome its scaly guardian
and bring some golden apples back."
Alcides set out for the river Po,
the favorite resort of Nereus.
The Old Man of the Sea would know
how best to prosecute his quest.
He paused midway across a rivulet
to rinse the dust from his parched gullet
when he beheld from where he knelt
a man in greaves, cuirass and helmet.
Cycnus was the son of Ares,
a fair-haired, Aryan barbarian
who detested fems and fairies,
as well as poets and their clan.

Prone to aggressive behavior
of every sort—looks, deeds and words,
Cycnus berated the stranger
in a flyting worthy of Welsh bards.
Alcides would have lost his cool
and clubbed him like a baby seal
if Ares hadn't saved the fool,
protecting Cycnus with his shield.
An expert at conducting duels
—one of his rôles as God of War—
Ares explained the basic rules
that govern an affaire d'honneur.
Brought up to snuff on protocol,
they were about to come to blows
when an explosion made them reel,
a bolt of lightning hurled by Zeus.
Zeus' displeasure duly noted,
the duel was canceled due to weather.
Cycnus skulked away and pouted.
Heracles continued on his venture.
As he approached the river Po,
he was arrested by a glimpse

of river nymphs lying exposed,
sunbathing their alluring limbs.
His eyes drank in their loveliness
until they called: "Why so aloof?"
Nymphs are proverbial for sex,
but this was his first solid proof.

Alcides rose to the occasion
and gave them what they hungered for.
After consummating their liaison,
they directed him to Nereus' lair.
Nereus' den was in a glade,
an alcove off the river's bend
where he would go to soak up shade,
a refuge from the daily grind.
Sacked out on his bulrush pallet,
the sea god snored, oblivious
to everything outside the thicket,
as if the world ceased to exist.
It was in just such a torpid state
Alcides found him and, foretold
of his aptitude for changing shape,
he pinned him in a wrestling hold.
The captive deity awoke.
Never sluggish on the uptake,
he fell back on his favorite trick:
assuming divers guises to escape.
He morphed into a waterfall,
a rushing wall of liquefaction.
Alcides bid the waves be still,
not taken in by the deception.
Nereus ransacked his repertoire,
becoming bear, boar, tiger beetle,
fish, stone, serpent, ice and fire,
earthworm, bullbat, cactus needle.

Throughout these protean mutations,
Alcides never loosed his grip,

clinging, despite his reservations,
tighter than Scrooge's money clip.
The shifty god, to slip the noose,
transformed himself into the twin
of Heracles, so the son of Zeus
was forced to wrestle his own clone!
He trounced his ersatz counterpart
for, though a master of disguise,
the merman couldn't counterfeit
the vibrant strength of Heracles.
The old roué threw in the towel.
Finding himself in narrow straits,
he vowed, on his release, to tell
the sacred garden's whereabouts.
The journey led through Libya,
he said, that snake-infested region,
and Egypt, where the sun god Ra
reigned over the priestly pantheon.
From there he must find Prometheus,
who introduced mankind to culture,
chained to a crag in the Caucasus,
his vitals gnawed by a hellish vulture.
The maverick Titan would provide
detailed directions to the garden
and explain what pitfalls to avoid
while gleaning Atlas' golden burden.
Alcides hopped an outbound freight
laden with sundry merchandise
to keep some sleazy plutocrat
in lampreys and Macassar grease.
The ship broke bulk in Libya
at a seaport called Cyrene,
which was, for Heracles' agenda,
as good a landing site as any.
He set out on his desert hadj;
no trek to Mecca for his God
but, though a worldly pilgrimage,
all noble acts conduce to good.
The hero came upon a shrine,

a temple roofed with human skulls,
a grinning parliament of bone
whose diet took the place of tiles.
As he stood, mutely mirating on
this curiously morbid edifice,
his eyes were inexorably drawn
to the architect himself—Antaeus.
Emerging from the inner sanctum,
the giant stepped into the light,
stooping to avoid the transom,
a handsome man for a troglodyte.
Antaeus lived in a sandstone cave,
subsisting on filet of lion,
spawn of Earth's incestuous love
for her grandson, the god Poseidon.

"Are you canon of this cathedral?"
the son of Zeus naively asked.
"The same. I built this tabernacle,"
Antaeus said, "and I conduct the Mass."
"And who are those upon the roof?"
Alcides asked with childlike candor.
"Poor pilgrims on the road of life,"
he sighed, "I did my best to succor."
The ogre's arrogant demeanor,
his proud and truculent expression
struck Alcides like a taser or
a stray pitch, rousing his suspicion.
"We have a custom in these parts."
Antaeus feigned a playful smile.
"When two athletic men cross paths,
they stop and wrestle without fail."
"Far be it from me to disobey
a custom sanctioned by long use.
Such things arise instinctively,"
said Heracles, "and come from Zeus."
Antaeus remained invincible
while touching Gaea—Mother Earth,
which is why it was so simple

to get free shingles for his church.
Laying aside their lion stoles
—their taste in clothing ran the same—
both men performed the rituals
befitting wrestlers in the ring.

But whereas Heracles used oil,
Antaeus rubbed himself with earth,
laving his skin with sandy soil
to add to his reserve of strength.
A few minutes into the bout,
the son of Zeus felt justified
in his mistrust. The truth will out:
Antaeus was intent on homicide.
"Not to worry!" quoth the raven.
Alcides can't get killed just yet.
The giant is a minor diversion,
what writers call a side exploit.
Using a maneuver he'd learned
in the wrestling school of Autolycus,
he threw Antaeus to the ground,
whence he arose with a rosy flush.
To wear his adversary down,
Alcides drew the fighting out
until Antaeus, on his own,
fell prostrate, rising fresher yet.
A hero of uncommon acumen,
Alcides accurately diagnosed
the ogre's clumsy clown routine
and hit upon a happy antidote.
He hugged aloft this Stone Age man,
this throwback to the Pleistocene
whose features would have charmed Rodin,
and crushed him like a used beer can.

There were still a few lacunae
in the carapace of the pagoda,
like truant teeth or alveolae.
Antaeus made a dandy cupola.

Zeus was venerated by a cult
as Ammon in a wayside temple.
Alcides, wishing to consult
his father, visited the oracle.
Mid swirling clouds of frankincense,
he craved a conference, one on one,
but All-father feared his radiance
would overwhelm and scorch his son.
Concealed beneath a wooly fleece
he'd swiped from an indignant ram,
Zeus chewed the fat with Heracles,
wearing the curved horns like a tam.
Around his head an aureole
boiled like aurora borealis
or some pyrotechnic girandole,
his own private ignis fatuus.
Some poet coined this ram device
to parody the pompous pride
that blasphemes instinct as a vice
and hides behind the cloak of God.
So rash St. Tom abruptly died
beholding God in an ecstasy,
as if to say that neither side
should gain unbridled mastery.

After his interview with Zeus,
Alcides departed the temple,
serene in its surreal oasis,
and embarked for Egypt's capital.
Some years before, the sullen sun
had scourged the land with baleful eye.
With swollen paunch and withered tongue,
God's cattle uttered a collective sigh.
The king of Egypt, Busiris,
consulted a Chaldean magus,
a soothsayer hailing from Cyprus
named Phrasius, aka "Caecus."[10]
The wizard said the drought would end
if there were put to death each year

some rootless tramp or footloose vagabond.
It was so ordered, starting with the seer.
Upon entering Wase, better known
to Greeks as Hecatompylon,
which translates "hundred-gated town,"
the fellahs fell upon Zeus' son.
Clapped in chains, he was paraded
before the teeming rank and file
to the scaffold to be decollated,
a spectacle to placate the canaille.
His brow was filleted with wool,
a formulaic psalm was raised,
attendants sprinkled him with meal,
the sacrificial axe was poised,

when Heracles burst his shackles,
slew Busiris and his goon squad.
Anubis and his junior jackals
welcomed them to the underworld.
Assuming the prerogative
accorded an heroic specimen
and those supposed a cut above
to lord it over lesser men,
Alcides changed the city's name
from Hecatompylon to Thebes,
after the source of his réclame
as champion of ancestral liberties.
At Rhodes, for lack of better fare,
he feasted on a farmer's ox.
The angry yeoman, from afar
flung curses interspersed with rocks.
From there he combed the Caucasus
in search of the secluded tor
where Zeus imprisoned Prometheus,
mankind's recalcitrant abettor.
A brutal twist on crucifixion,
the Titan's torment was extreme
compared to Sisyphus or Ixion
and other paragons of crime.

Chained with metal cuffs and pitons
against the cliff's unyielding face,
a vulture came each day to feed on
his viscera, devouring gobs of flesh.

Threading his way among the hills,
led more by instinct than design,
weaving a skein of snail-like trails,
Alcides tracked man's benefactor down.
Although the setting was austere,
remote from public hub or hearth
where patrons go to banish care
and spend the surplus of the heart,
their converse was as debonair
as any close-knit coterie
that ever met to share the air
with luminaries of the clerisy.
Alcides asked what brought him there.
Was he a monitory sacrifice?
Was it the fabled rape of fire
or was his punishment a cruel caprice?

"I never smuggled fire from Heaven,
fire by Zeus's will to me was given.
All we accomplish in the world below
is only what He wishes to bestow.
The suffering for men I have endured,
long ages of good fortune has ensured.
Some, He dooms to prematurely die
that blessings on the rest can multiply.
Your journey here was also prophesied,
the man by whom Prometheus was freed."

Just then a buzzard wheeled in sight,
tacking and veering in the wind,
surfing the thermals like a kite.
Its wing-beats made a husky, rustling sound.
"Bruno is dropping by for lunch,"
Prometheus remarked sardonically.

"For once I have a sneaking hunch
he'll wish he'd ordered in today."
Reeling tighter with every turn
the perns of its contracting gyre,
the infernal bird's flight pattern
passed within yards of their eyrie.
Heracles, with seamless gestures,
loaded, aimed, and fired a rocket
that burst in a fanfare of feathers
when wooden bolt and ornithopter met.
The bird let out a savage cry
and spiralled downward like a leaf.
Prometheus pronounced the eulogy:
"Good riddance! May he rot in peace."
Availing himself of a secret
vouchsafed back at the oasis,
a form of address more sacred
than the corn god of Eleusis,
Heracles obtained permission
to set the arch-recusant free,
reminding Zeus-pater of Chiron,
who wanted shut of immortality.

The wise old Centaur shuffled off
his immortal coil, for he had borne
life's slings and arrows long enough
and yearned to pass beyond death's bourne.
Heracles yanked the metal spikes,
using his club to jar them loose,
swingeing with sturdy hammer-strokes,
thus setting the stage for Aeschylus.
The gentle giant, now unbound
and deathless,[11] warned his ex-tormentor
to drop his suit for Thetis' hand
lest he beget his own successor.
Savoring his newfound freedom
after an aeon under duress,
one thing alone remained undone:
repaying Heracles for his largess.

The Titan, reclining on a stone,
dilated on the shortest route
to the garden of the setting sun
and how to filch the golden fruit.
No one spurned that turf before him
but Uruk's king, intrepid Gilgamesh,
whose quest to question Utnapishtim
led to the temperate bower of Shamash.
For days on end Alcides faced
the barren waste without the taste
of food or water, trudging west,
his gaunt cheeks hollow as a ghost.

Sporadic tufts of stoic greenery
intruded on the sabulous sea,
infringing on the sterile scenery
till dunes gave way to luscious lea.
The air grew vibrant with the song
of birds, the murmuring of leaves.
A vernal ichor, young and strong,
made zaftig earth's eclectic entities.
He abutted on a crenellated wall,
a bulwark reared of rough-hewn megaliths
with barbicans to guard against assault,
though here were neither Gauls nor Visigoths.
Such monumental piles of stone
have mostly been reserved for those
whose dainty nates graced a throne,
their egos perilously grandiose.
Tracing the wall's periphery,
he came to a quaint embrasure,
a portal of azure porphyry
with an elaborate entablature.
He gave the door a gentle push,
surprised at finding it ajar.
It swiveled open with a whoosh
as wind swept through the aperture.
The fields unfurled before his eyes
were named for the renowned Hesperides,

praised in the lays of other days
as Dilmun, Eden, Asgard, Paradise.

Atlas' daughters roamed the meadows,
weaving chaplets to adorn their tresses,
trolling airs and three-part operettas
as sweet as honey from Hymettus.
Spring, that Dionysian season,
was perpetual, reason being
the garden's pivotal location,
beyond the range of winter's fang.
Ladon was the garden's sentry,
a reptile of outstanding parts,
a member of the dragon gentry,
past master of the mantic arts.
Crossing the intervening croft,
Alcides reached earth's finisterre,
where Atlas held the world aloft,
though what he stood on isn't clear.
Heracles was frank with Atlas,
explaining in plebeian phrases
what he wanted with the apples
and why he'd made his anabasis.
"Why stick your neck out?" Atlas said.
"That dragon's like a pet to me.
He's sweet as lamb's milk when he's fed.
I'd fetch the apples if my hands were free."
Rather than face the dragon's wrath
and slay so mannerly a creature,
Alcides chose to prop the earth
while Atlas took a little breather.

Putting his shoulder to the wheel,
he hoisted the telluric sphere.
If Heracles had dropped the ball,
life might have ended then and there.

Atlas lolled about the meadow,
feeling like a pardoned felon,

lounging in a live oak's shadow,
munching chunks of watermelon.
This taste of the dolce vita
fired Atlas with a love of gold.
A life of leisure is sweeter
than playing caryatid to the world.
Instead of dealing with the dragon,
he got the apples from his daughters,
who plucked them to relieve the sagging
branches, hoarding them like staters.
Atlas, returning with the booty,
told Heracles peremptorily
he felt it was his bounden duty
to take the apples to Mycenae.
Alcides said he understood
and only asked the Titan leave
to put a cushion on his head
for reasons easy to conceive.
It seemed a sensible request,
so Atlas graciously complied
and briefly reassumed his post
after laying the fruit aside.

Heracles swept up the plunder
and booked without a backward glance.
Atlas recognized his blunder
and reviled him from a distance.
His journey seemed incredible
to the simple folks back home until
he showed them the inedible
fruit. Even then most doubted still.
Eurystheus admired the apples,
but they had a bad track record.
Anyone who touched the globules
was jinxed by the goddess Discord.
He foisted them on Heracles,
who fobbed them off on Athena.
She passed them to the 'sperides,
who socked them away for Hera.

Book XII

It would exceed the skill of any god
to mete out perfect justice,
to weigh our actions, good and bad,
and appropriately curse or bless.
Is there a reckoning in Heaven
to calculate our souls' arrears,
decide how hot to set the oven
or where to hang the Rembrandts and Vermeers?
If God were half as critical
of us as we are of each other,
we may as well go straight to Hell
and skip the Last Assize. Why bother?
And on that subject, Hell is where
Eurystheus sent Heracles anon.
He'd heard no one came back from there
and that's what he was banking on.
His twelfth and most atrocious labor,
the copestone of his magnum opus,
was to subjugate Hell's gatekeeper,
the tricephalic watchdog Cerberus.
Descending to the netherworld
was a dicey proposition.
It wouldn't do to go there cold
without the juju of religion.

The martyrdom of Zagreus
was regarded as a sacrament
by the priesthood of Eleusis
in their yearly reenactment.
Zagreus' death and resurrection
symbolically embodied truths
concerning Hell and transmigration
profoundly simple, yet abstruse.
Admission to this esoteric sect[12]
was seen as a cachet of honor
and was limited to the elect,

Athenians of spotless character.
Alcides sought to be admitted but,
not only was he not a citizen,
his scutcheon wasn't without blot.
Centauromachy left a crimson stain.
The residency objection
was laid to rest by Pylius,
who agreed to adopt Zeus' son,
reversing his alien status.
The charge of shedding Centaur blood
was disposed of by Eumolpus,
a member of the ancient brotherhood
who exorcised the pesky incubus.

The season of the festival
rolled round with apodictic certainty.
The mystagogue was masterful
and drew the curtain on eternity.
Freed of the matrices that bind
our finite minds to space and time,
seeing in every particle of wind
a partner in an abstract paradigm,
Heracles embarked for Tartarus,
taking stock of his adoptive home,
its groves, Piraeus and Acropolis,
the scene of so much drama yet to come.
He made his harrowing descent
from a cave on Cape Taenarus
at Greece's southernmost extent,
a papilla of the Peloponnesus.
The tunnel's darkness was profound.
Coiling like some monstrous annelid
that burrows blindly underground,
through miles of rock the channel led.
Erupting from the crude crevasse
coated in crud from head to foot,
Alcides felt about as cuddly as
a sewer rat embalmed in creosote.

The fissure issued on a fen,
an esplanade of asphodel
where bullfrogs belched in unison,
the misty vestibule to Hell.

Above his head the cavern dome
soared like a stratosphere of stone,
high as the nave of Nôtre Dame,
a roost no gargoyle would disdain.
Alcides plodded through the slough
till stymied by the Styx nearby,
whose turbid current, thick as glue,
furnished gods a term to swear by.
He hadn't stood there long before
a figure hailed him from afar.
The pilot poled the boat ashore.
It was Charon, angling for a fare.
Back then, a proper burial
was not a boon to be derided.
Loved ones secreted an obol
under the tongues of those who died.
Souls with coins upon arrival,
Charon whisked across the river,
while those without the wherewithal
were barred from Tartarus forever.
Charon was a twerp, a reprobate,
a putrid flake of human flotsam,
a scrawny scrap of buzzard bait,
a stooge, a fugitive from Sodom.
On closer view, Hell's gondolier
became aware of his mistake.
He scrutinized his passenger:
the son of Zeus was too opaque.

He said: "I cain't give you a ride.
Only haints can cross this river.
O' course, if you committed suicide,
I might see fit to reconsider."

The muscleman was in no mood
to humor this demented twit.
He scowled, advancing as he did,
and Charon stammered: "I sssee fffit!"
He took a seat aboard the bark,
which rode inordinately low
as Charon urged the scurvy ark
across the river's ebon flow.
A gaggle of ghosts had gathered at
the wharf where Charon moored his boat
to greet whatever guests he brought,
whether lowly serfs or souls of note.
When Heracles set foot on shore
and stood erect, the spectres fled
like Aztecs fleeing a conquistador,
as if they weren't already dead.
Beyond a featureless expanse
of brown, a field of withered furze,
Hell's walls and towers rose, immense,
a huge necropolis ablaze with fires.
Starting across the sombre heath,
Alcides thought the coast was clear
until Medusa blocked his path,
the Gorgon with the petrifying stare.

He drew his sword and looked askance,
afraid of her enchanted glance.
The snaky tresses on her sconce
waved to and fro in captivating dance.
Hermes witnessed these proceedings.
The god of mischief couldn't hide
his glee at such outlandish doings,
a mortal locked in combat with a shade.
He gave away Medusa's ruse
—having enjoyed his fill of farce—
exposing her for what she was:
a mere eidolon void of force.
He wished his agnate happy trails
and revved up his talaria,

i.e. the wings that fledged his heels,
then sped from Hell's malaria.
As Heracles approached the gate
of Hades and Persephone,
he met with yet another wraith,
a more beneficent epiphany.
A golden soldier sallied forth,
a paladin in costly armor.
His wealth suggested noble birth,
a prince to judge from his demeanor.
The soldier's free and easy stride
betrayed his youthful confidence.
Here was a lion, ruler of the pride,
a knight who counted caution cowardice.

Alcides, ever vigilant
to head off mischief, drew his bow,
uncertain if his visitant
would turn out friend or deadly foe.
The hoplite halted far enough
away to forestall the missile
and, letting out a boisterous laugh,
launched into a brief recital.
"Rest easy Heracles! Why squander
the Hydra's blood? It has no virtue
against the dead. Those who wander
these fields are powerless to hurt you.
The supple tongue of gossip has
relayed Meleager down the years.
My name's been often cited as
a subject for the public's ears.
When Artemis unleashed a boar
on Calydon, her punishment
of Oeneus, my regal father for
lax sacrifice, I led the hunt.
I assembled the very cream
of sportsmen from among the locals,
including Atalanta, whom
I loved, and my maternal uncles.

The boar was a real monsterator.
The whetted edges of its tushes
would have shredded us like paper
had it rushed us from the bushes.

It ran, preferring flight to fight,
and left the rest of us behind,
but Atalanta, faster on her feet,
kept up and gored the rampant swine.
The tusker turned, a study in
demonic rage; no squealing shoat,
but hardened hate, and it was then
I drove my own spear down its throat.
To Atalanta I gave the boar's
head as a token of affection.
My uncles, chauvinistic boors,
wrested it from her possession.
I killed the rascals out of hand,
in retaliation for which act,
my mother lit the sacred brand
to which my lifespan was attached."
Meleager ended his narration.
Dispensing with amenities,
they struck up a conversation
revealing myriad affinities.
In the course of their palaver,
which grew increasingly familiar,
Alcides offered, as a favor,
to wed Meleager's spinster sister.[13]
The heroes, thick as thieves by now,
had worked their way back toward the gate,
where Heracles broke off the interview,
dumbfounded by the shocking scene thereat.

Two men were fettered side by side
in chairs designed exclusively
to toast their brains—electrified.
The captives writhed convulsively.
Behind the tortured grimaces,

Alcides recognized the deuce
as fellow Argonauts of his,
Kings Theseus and Pirithous.
The hapless duo came to Hell
to lure Persephone away,
but caught the devil when they fell
afoul of Hades' watchful eye.
Recognizing the son of Zeus,
the pair reached out imploringly.
Heracles seized hold of Theseus
and wrenched him free accordingly.
He tried to rescue Pirithous
but that's where Hades drew the line.
He shook Hell with a force so fierce,
Alcides had to leave his pal behind.
The hero came upon a man
pinned beneath a stone so ample,
it might have figured in the plan
of a dolmen or druidic temple.
Like Caiaphas, Ascalaphus
had made a faulty judgment call.
The charge was base in either case,
for truth demands a lofty soul.

When Hades first abducted her,
Persephone eschewed all food
till, to better stave off hunger,
she chewed a pomegranate seed.
Ascalaphas, to her disgust,
kept watch and caught her in the act,
and when the issue was discussed,
he testified to that effect.
Eating in Hell is tantamount
to forfeiting the right to leave,
no matter whether the amount
is fifty pounds or an hors d'oeuvre.
Persephone's clandestine meal
had destined her to spend a third
of every year in Hades' hall

below the surface of the world.
To avenge her daughter, Demeter
petitioned Dis to sequester
Ascalaphas beneath the boulder,
which he did to conciliate her.
Ignoring Hades' jurisdiction,
Alcides heaved aside the stone,
a random act of compassion,
misguided though it may have been.
The spirits overcame their fear
so well, meanwhile, that some began
to hover uncomfortably near,
their faces uniformly woebegone.

Nothing elates the sullen shades
like a few slugs of mammal blood.
A short way off, a herd of Hades'
plethoric cattle munched the cud.
Choosing a zaftig specimen,
Alcides killed the fatted calf
by severing its jugular vein,
catching the runoff in a trough.
The spooks, converging on the pool
like Catholics at Communion,
imbibed the blood, which made them feel
alive again, a soothing delusion.
Menoetes, Hades' herdsman, got
all het up over the illicit
slaughter of his hand-fed cosset
and angrily threw down the gauntlet.
Facing a stranger in a rage
whose conduct seemed a shade outré,
Alcides did what any sage
would do: he broke his ribs straightway.
The altercation at the gate
attracted Hades' comely spouse,
who came out to investigate
what all the ruckus was about.

Persephone adapted well
to Hell, though wed against her will,
secure in Hades' love. Why else
would he have plucked her from the hill?

The Queen of Darkness intervened,
pleading on Menoetes' behalf.
The calf, she said, was barely weaned,
an orphan he had nursed himself.
Heracles released the shepherd,
acceding to the queen's request.
She then subpoenaed Hell's landlord
to welcome their flamboyant guest.
The ruler of the netherworld,
for all his pomp and circumstance,
burned rubber when his lover called,
a god who understood romance.
When he received his wife's summons,
Hades declared a brief recess
and joined Persephone at once,
still draped in his gown of office.
Devoted husband though he was,
malefactors feared his gavel
in his capacity as final judge,
worse than death or any devil.
"To what do we owe this pleasure?"
asked Hades with an evanescent smile.
Heracles replied: "I need a favor.
I'd like to borrow Cerberus awhile."
A second, longer lasting grin
redrew the districts of his face
as Hades gently stroked his chin.
"You're free to borrow Cerberus,"
he said, "if you can subjugate
the brute bare-handed, one on one.
You'll find him stationed at the gate
just opposite the river Acheron."

When Heracles neared the entry
where Cerberus was on alert
as a rough and ready sentry,
the mastiff raged as if berserk.
The hero watched just out of reach
as the hound thrashed wildly on its leash.
Its three heads gnashed serrated teeth
and strained to lacerate his flesh.
Protected by his lion mail
from all the snakes along its back
and poison dragon of a tail,
he flung his arms around its neck.
He pacified the creature by
steadily tightening his grip,
reducing its oxygen supply,
inducing asphyxial sleep.
Heracles carried Cerberus
back to the surface world of light,
his last debt to Eurystheus,
whose reason foundered at the sight.
He swore undying enmity
toward Heracles, eternal war
to root out his posterity—
whatever bore his signature.

A bestial nature is our curse,
but thanks to a capacious brain
that sometimes mellows jealous curs
to Cynics, men are more humane.

Book XIII

A hero's character is struck
from the anvil of adversity.
He learns to weather every shock.
Tough luck is his university.
After completing his labors,
Heracles returned to his estate
where his Theban friends and neighbors
lionized him like a head of state.
He tried to forget, but couldn't,
the stigma of his derelict days.
Loneliness kindled the dormant
ember of remorse into a blaze.
The only way to allay his mind
was to embark afresh on life
and leave his guilty past behind
by breaking in a brand new wife.
Word reached his ear that Eurytus,
who'd taught him how to use a bow
—a skilful marksman, but vainglorious—
was in the market for a son-in-law.
His daughter Iole was in
her apple years, a budding rose.
Her looks affected men like wine:
she made them giddy and verbose.

Contestants for the beauty's hand
competed in a shooting meet
against the master archer and
his sons, but none had won her yet.
Overrun with beaus and eros,
Iole reaped no advantage,
mewed behind a veil of arrows,
a songbird in a soundproof cage.
Before Alcides studied wooing,
there was Megara to consider.
Their union led to his undoing
and launched his Übermensch career.

Heracles bestowed Megara
on his nephew Iolaus
in a private marriage cere-
mony tastefully unostentatious.
Then, clutching his beloved bow,
a weapon only he could bend,
made from a seasoned piece of yew,
he took to the open road again.
Eurytus was Oechalia's prince,
a sportsman, to the manner born;
a playboy noted for his pranks.
His father doddered on the throne.
His theory was that any man
who proved himself at archery
would make a better husband than
some nebbish with a pedigree.

A maven of the martial art,
he taught his four sons how to shoot
till they were only less expert
than he was, owing to their youth.
It was against this mise en scène
that Heracles breezed into town
and threw his Stetson in the ring
to win a kewpie doll to call his own.
The belle maintained a high profile
to foster keener competition,
flashing her most beguiling smile.
Street vendors jockeyed for position.
The tournament got under way.
The suitors were a motley crew.
Eurytus was dismayed to see
his former pupil in the queue.
The amphitheater was full
of voluble, rambunctious Greeks
eager to view the spectacle
and cheer or jeer like maniacs.
Eurytus addressed the target
and, after a dramatic pause,

let fly an almost perfect shot,
igniting rapturous applause.
When everyone resumed their seat,
his sons approached the firing line,
but couldn't match their father's feat.
Then came the suitors' turn to shine.

With every arrow they released,
the princess quivered from the stress.
Each time another missive missed,
her heart played bebop in her chest.
When Heracles came up to bat,
he checked the windage once or twice,
then notched an arrow on the gut
and fixed the target in his sights.
The bolt exploded from the bow,
a burst of urgent energy,
ripping like a pissed neutrino
through the defenseless effigy.
The audience was galvanized,
hysterical as rhesus monkeys
on crack or laboratory mice
convulsed by six volt batteries.
The prince was noticeably peeved.
His brow was clouded by a cowl
that shrouded like a winter's eve
his visage with a brumal scowl.
The losing suitors left the field
to let the dark prince and his foil
sustain the farce as best they could
and wow the groundlings with a duel.
And what a monumental match
it was. What brio! What sangfroid!
A clash of Titans. What panache!
What chutzpah! What *je ne sais quois*!

Alcides differed from the prince
in that, while Eurytus could hit

a bull's eye within half an inch,
the son of Zeus could geld a gnat.
The outcome was beyond dispute.
The hoi polloi were overjoyed.
The underdog had won his suit.
The prince was royally annoyed.
His vanity demanded wine
to dull the anguish in his heart,
which was like pouring gasoline
on a fire to retard the heat.
When Heracles showed up to claim
his prize, the prince was in his cups.
The grape juice had inflamed his brain
and scathing words escaped his lips.
"I repudiate the shooting match!
I'll never permit my daughter
to furnish you a second batch
of blue-eyed cherubim to slaughter!
I rue the day I taught you how
to shoot a bow. You're just a thug.
If I knew then what I know now,
I would have crushed you like a bug!
I banish you from Oechalia!
If you don't leave the city by
this afternoon, I swear I'll kill you!
Child-murderers deserve no mercy."

The hero wasn't quick enough
to see the forest for the trees
and let himself be driven off.
The bastard bum-rushed Heracles.
The son of Zeus no sooner left
than cattle were stolen from Eurytus,
who blamed Alcides for the theft,
when the true culprit was Autolycus.
Heracles' plight aroused the sympathy
of Eurytus's eldest son.
Iphitus maintained that Iole
had been legitimately won.

He undertook an embassy
to bring about a rapprochement,
a little shuttle diplomacy
to promote a spirit of detente.
He followed Heracles to Thebes
and asked the man of might to join
in tracking down the cattle thieves,
too young to do the job alone.
It must have struck Alcides odd
to be solicited for aid
by the hostile camp, but if it did,
he overlooked it and agreed.
When Heracles correctly guessed
he was suspected of the theft,
he waxed indignant at his guest
and hurled him from a minaret.[14]

After the death of Iphitus,
he was stricken with an illness
and betook himself to Pylus
to be purged of guilt by Neleus.
But Neleus denied him succor
lest he anger Eurytus, his ally.
Ditto his sons, except Nestor,
who treated him hospitably.
Nestor convinced Deiphobus,
who reigned in nearby Amyclae,
to purify the son of Zeus
and cure him of his malady.
The outward symptoms abated,
but the root cause of his distress
refused to be deracinated,
i.e. a conscience poisoned by remorse.
Tormented by macabre dreams,
a private hell inside his skull,
his mind replayed the frightened screams
his children uttered as they fell.
He resorted to the oracle
of Delphi where the Pythoness

sat perched above a spiracle,
inhaling trance-inducing gas.
When Heracles approached the shrine,
the Sibyl's answer was severe,
conditioned by an endless line
of whining clients at her door.

"Who do I look like, Morpheus?
Am I responsible for dreams?
Your temper got you in this mess
and now you're paying for your crimes."
Nettled by her petulant tone,
Alcides said: "If you won't help,
I'll build a temple of my own
and dispense the oracles myself."
He entered the penetralia
and carried off the sacred hoard
that lay within, inter alia,
the stool the priestess occupied.
Apollo, with omniscient eye,
observed this act of sacrilege
and scheduled an epiphany
to check the threat to his prestige.
The stool became their cynosure.
As Heracles and Phoebus fought,
Zeus registered his displeasure
by hurling lightning at their feet.
The tripod is a metaphor
for the incessant tug of war
between the miter and the sword,
the sacred and the secular.
The shock therapy did the trick.
Cowed by Big Daddy's power play,
Alcides put the Delphic relics back.
Apollo pardoned his lèse-majesté.

Positioned by the Omphalos
—the navel of the universe—
the Sibyl, in her vatic voice,

evoked a verse from the abyss.
"To appease Tisiphone's wrath,
you must be auctioned as a slave
and compensate the dead man's wraith
with the blood-money you receive."
Alcides, guided to the sale
by Hermes, who brokered the deal,
was purchased by Queen Omphale,
inscrutable behind her veil.
To propitiate Iphitus,
heraldic Hermes took the gold
and offered it to Eurytus,
but he rejected their wergild.
When King Tmolus bit the dust,
Lydia's queen was seventeen,
but her Attic salt and classic bust
secured her title to the throne.
She loved her husband dearly but
she was still young and full of fun,
too doggone sexy to be celibate
or wear a widow's weeds for long.
The men who courted her conversed
ad nauseam about their wealth
and bored her after hour the first,
as if they thought of nothing else.

Omphale, from her palanquin,
saw Heracles on the auction block
and had a visceral reaction.
His sculpted muscles made her quake.
She had a vacant stall to fill
and Heracles was just the stud
to give the lonely queen a thrill,
a stallion valued for his seed.
Their romance was proverbial:
two troubled souls in search of love,
whose weaknesses exactly parallel
a strength the other has abundance of.
The queen, clad in his lion skin,

made Heracles don lingerie
and help her servants spin their yarn,
as this cliché is helping me.
There's a revealing anecdote,
an episode that clearly shows
the lovers were so intimate,
they often wore each other's clothes.
One day the hircine deity
was munching leaves abstractedly
upon a hill when who should he
espy but Heracles and Omphale.
The minx's titillating laugh,
her breasts, provocatively bare,
so round, so firm, so fully packed,
lit Pan's libido like a flare.

He stalked them to a summerhouse,
a furnished grotto in the woods
where frisky couples could carouse
far from the ballyhoo of crowds.
Emboldened by the privacy
afforded by the cave, the queen
shook off the yoke of modesty
and gave her fantasies free rein.
Swapping costumes and personas,
she caricatured Heracles,
strutting like Miles Gloriosus.
Alcides shimmied in her silk chemise.
After ringing the changes on
their charade of trading sexes,
they prorogued their steamy session
and retired to separate couches.
Darkness, confederate of crime,
concealed Pan as he crept inside
the chamber, quiet as a mime,
to taste the love broad day forbade.
His furtive fingers felt the fur
of Heracles' protective pelt.
His bowels were paralyzed with fear.

The satyr damn near soiled hisself!
Badly unnerved, yet undeterred,
the cashmere Casanova turned
to find the idol he adored,
the Beatrice for whom he burned.

He fumbled clumsily about
as blind as Homer's bust until
he stubbed his foot against a couch
whose occupant was swathed in silk.
Like Moses, he believed the land
of milk and honey beckoned just
ahead. The kingdom was at hand;
the rapture had arrived at last.
He slyly eased beneath the sheet,
but when he tried to dip his wick,
the burly hero cocked his foot
and sent him sprawling with a kick.
The rumpus wakened Omphale,
who lit a lamp. The lantern's ray
exposed Pan's phallic fallacy
and made the madcap lovers gay.
Thereafter, the embarrassed lord
of forest dwellers, out of spite,
let slip no chance to spread the word
Alcides was a closet transvestite.
As therapeutic as it was
for Heracles to get in touch
with his softer side, hero-wise,
he also did some macho stuff.
He undertook a one man program
to root out nihilistic vermin
at Omphale's request, a pogrom.
Brute force is still the best sermon.

As he crisscrossed the ancient state
to domesticate the naked ape,
two gnomes adept at changing shape,
disguised as flies disturbed his sleep.

The Cercopes were malicious elves
who regarded morals as a hoax,
enabling skeptics like themselves
to skim the wealth of working folks.
They pestered Heracles because
his presence in the neighborhood
was bad for business and the buzz
would ultimately drive him mad.
Their machinations came to naught.
As they flew sorties round his bed,
he intercepted them one night
and made them ditch the fly façade.
He tied the midgets to a pole
and hauled them, hanging upside down,
toward Ephesus to cast in jail,
some rat-infested castle dungeon.
The inverted image of his buns,
brown from exposure to the sun,
bobbing like casaba melons,
amused the cretins where they hung.
Alcides asked the evil elves
what they were cachinnating at,
and they fired back: "Your ass! What else?"
He had to laugh himself at that.

This unexpected interlude
of asinine hilarity
put Heracles in so good a mood,
he let the imbeciles go free.
On the lower slope of a ravine
lived a scrap of flesh named Syleus.
He manufactured table wine,
but his methods were unscrupulous.
He'd wait for some unlucky schmoe
to shuffle past his house when lo,
he'd rough them up and make them hoe
his vines, row after miserable row.
He bit off more than he could chew
when he assailed the son of Zeus,

who used his hoe to lay him low
and tore his vines up by the roots.
Another malefactor who
deserves dishonorable mention
is Lityerses, whose éclat is due
to an atrocious disposition.
Each autumn, when the corn was ripe,
he'd whet the curved blade of his scythe.
Then, snath in hand, he'd mow his crop
and bind the sheaves, swath after swath.
When some lone individual
passed by, he'd force him to compete
in a cruel harvest ritual,
a reap off or Wimbledon of wheat.

His victims were provided with
a scythe and at the go-ahead,
they vainly vied to slash a path
more swiftly than Lityerses did.
He lashed the losers with a scourge
and beheaded them with a stroke
of his sickle. Then, chanting a dirge,
he stashed the corpses in a stook.
A murmur reached Alcides' ear
too widespread to be mere rumor
about a kind of Jack the Reaper,
a Mack the Scythe or cereal killer.
He traced the story to its source
and found the farmer at his trade.
Lityerses challenged him to race
and Heracles complaisantly complied.
The contest was no fable then,
no frozen frieze or formal ode,
but a struggle to the death between
two alpha males in combat mode.
The killer set a brutal pace.
"He'll fold, they always do." he thought,
but Heracles was on his arse
like white on rice or flies on sh~t.

Lityerses started losing ground
and so, no stranger to deceit,
attacked the hero from behind
to cheat his way out of defeat.

His cunning plan concealed a flaw.
Before he was able to strike,
Heracles beat him to the draw
and severed his devious neck.
He stuffed the body in a shock
and flung the bundle in the river.
The head he mounted on a pike,
a spoil for crows to quarrel over.
Next, he visited the island
of Doliche, where he ran across
a carcass washed up on the sand
he recognized as Icarus.
He buried the remains and gave
a eulogy before the stela
he carved to mark the shallow grave,
rechristening the isle Icaria.
Daedalus, the Greek Edison,
still surfing thermals overhead,
saw Heracles inter his son
and later repaid his good deed.
Returning to his atelier
and his beloved esoterica
—eclectic genius junk, e.g.
prisms, astrolabes, etcetera,
the mastermind cast a statue
of his legendary friend, a
facsimile using the cire-perdue
method to adorn Pisa's plaza.

The replica was so lifelike
that Heracles one night mistook
it for a prowler in the dark
and brained the icon with a rock.

The queen, proud mother of a brood
of budding heirs and heiresses,
concluded she could now afford
to dispense with his stud services.
Omphale freed her favorite slave.
Promoting him to Chief of Staff,
she placed him on administrative leave
and gave him an extravagant sendoff.

Book XIV

Of thee I sing, **WAR**, bitter battles
in words that wouldn't displease Homer.
My inn is free of clay and wattles
that put blasé readers in a coma.
Cured of demonic possession
by the love of a good woman,
Heracles turned his attention
to revenge against Laomedon.
He hopped a boxcar to Salamis
where Telamon was bibbing wine
and roasting mammal carcasses
with friends to entertain his pregnant queen.
In keeping with so fine a feast,
Heracles rose to propose a toast,
lifting his chalice like a priest
when he elevates the wine and host.
"Lord Zeus, send Telamon a son,"
he prayed with charismatic zeal,
"as tough as this Nemean lion skin."
A screaming eagle sealed the deal.
As if in response to Zeus' bird,
Periboea withdrew from the crowd
to her boudoir, where she delivered
baby Ajax, a modified Nimrod.

Spurning the perquisites of peace,
the tepid domestic routine,
Telamon teamed up with Heracles
to take on Troy's renegade king.
It's uncertain whether the force
Heracles gathered was large or small;
whether eighteen ships of fifty oars
each or six light craft and few men withal.
More clear-cut is that Iolaus
joined his uncle's expedition,
as did Oicles and Peleus,
and Deimachus the Boeotian.

Unlike opera or television,
no fanfare greeted his return;
no tragic chorus loitered on
the shore chanting in unison.
The fleet no sooner landed than
he spearheaded the invasion
in a play to take down the Trojan
padrone and his organization.
Laomedon woke in a sweat.
A skeleton, emblem of death,
was mowing a field of ripe wheat
as the dreamer knelt in its path.
It didn't take the pince-nez of Freud
to see the dream was a bad omen
with hysteria reigning right outside,
thanks to Heracles and his yeomen.

He merged with the bewildered herd.
Diverting a fraction from flight to fight,
he led them, armed with fire and sword,
shoreward to bushwhack the Greek fleet.
Only one person stood between
the Trojan posse comitatus
and the beaked warships, but that one
was Oicles, and that made all the difference.
Anyone dumb enough to try
and buffalo him found out pronto,
he was the road less traveled by,
a cross between John Wayne and Ivanhoe.
Laomedon's lackeys attacked him,
but found themselves so sore bestead
—Oicles so adroitly rebuked 'em—
they wished they hadda stood in bed.
Heracles was thoroughly irked
to see his armada in jeopardy
and his hard-earned reputation burked
by Laomedon's two-bit treachery.
Recalling all his warriors,
they hurriedly retraced their steps

to rout the Trojan saboteurs,
racing full bore to save the ships.
When he saw his crewmates en route,
Oicles' heart was infused with fresh heat,
but his Marseillaise was cut short
when Laomedon cleft his occiput.

With Oicles out of the picture,
the Trojans had free rein until,
falling on them like a raptor,
Heracles et al. flew down the hill.
Dardan resistance was token.
Laomedon retooled his strategy.
While his foes focused on the smoking
ships, he retook control of Troy.
The damage inflicted on the fleet
and the death of fierce Oicles let loose
a Phlegethon of Greek anger and grief.
Heracles' wrath reached critical mass.
They would rather have perished in
a mutual conflagration
than be robbed of the satisfaction
of reducing the town to a ruin.
Assailing the fort a fortiori
in search of a doorway to glory,
they prayed that some unborn Firdausi
would immortalize them in story.
Telamon was first to infiltrate
the bulwark where crumbling mortar
afforded purchase for his feet,
traversing it lightly as a stair.
Incensed that one of his own men
had entered Troy ahead of him,
Heracles shagged after Telamon,
sword drawn, to carve him like a ham.

Perceiving his breach of etiquette
and being attached to his bowels,

Telamon fell back on mother wit
to preserve his imperiled entrails.
He gathered at a rapid rate
some rubble providence no doubt
had strewn there for his benefit
and engineered an ad hoc ziggurat.
This maneuver threw a spanner
in Alcides' murder-meter.
Perplexed by Telamon's behavior,
he subdued his rampant anger.
"Are you insane?" he asked. "Not at all.
I raced ahead to raise a shrine
to Heracles, Supreme in Battle."
Appeased, the son of Zeus moved on.
The Trojan king was ripe for death.
His crimes had long ago surpassed
the yardstick karma's measured with
and checkout time had come at last.
Heracles spied Laomedon
and, never one to supinely let slip
such an auspicious occasion,
the hero let a vicious arrow rip.
The momentum from the bullet
spun the kingpin like a dreydl.
He stumbled toward the parapet
and tumbled all the way to hell.

The king's fall from grace aborted
the war. The Argives divvied up
the spoils. Hesione was awarded
to Telamon as his loving cup.
All Laomedon's sons were slain
but one so, before leaving Troy,
Heracles set Priam on the throne,
bestowing sovereignty on a boy.
Their high spirits quickly faded
thanks to Hera's intervention,
for the son of Zeus was hated
by the goddess with a passion.

Jump-starting Jupiter's libido
with promises of erotic games,
she lured him to a quaint gazebo
where Hypnos waited in the wings.
As they dallied in the aromatic
verdure of the charming arbor,
the god of sleep performed his shtick,
anesthetizing Zeus with slumber.
When Mighty Jove was comatose,
Hera loosed a tempest so relentless,
it almost swamped Alcides' boats
and drove them to the coast of Cos.
The Coans pelted them with stones,
mistaking them for marauders,
but the battle-hardened veterans
threw them back and slew their leaders.

Upon awaking, Zeus looked out
and saw his son under assault,
remote from his intended route,
and divined who was behind it all.
"Hera!" Zeus stormed, "Where is Hera?!"
and flew from his couch in a rage.
The goddess absconded in terror
to avoid the brunt of his rampage.
But there was no hiding this time,
for Jove was omniscient. Beside,
she had really stepped over the line
and he wanted a piece of her hide.
Bellowing like a bull walrus,
Zeus galumphed across Olympos
to heap invective on his spouse
and reassert his Alpha status.
The other gods were mortified
at such a sordid episode,
but when they tried to intercede,
Zeus turned his ire on them instead.
"I'll teach you not to interfere,"
he snarled and, seizing Apollo

by his thick mane of flaxen hair,
hurled him through a nearby window.
Hephaestus paid a heavy toll
for helping Hera. Flung by the heel,
he spun through space a day until
the isle of Lemnos broke his fall.

When Hera was apprehended,
Zeus hung her like a side of beef
from heaven's dome with golden thread,
twin anvils dangling from her feet.
Before the advent of humanity,
the only entities were Sky
and Earth. To break the monotony,
Ouranos and Ge got freaky.
This union led to unforeseen
ramifications, e.g. children.
Ouranos locked up their offspring
in Tartaros, to Ge's chagrin.
When Kronos was mature enough,
Ge told her son the time had come
to take revenge on Ouranos
by lopping off his sovereign schlong.
She gave the lad a Pop-sickle
and contrived a cunning ambush.
When Ouranos pulled out his pickle,
Kronos chopped it off with relish.
The fertile foam created when
the disjecta membrum splashed down
like Mark Spitz in the Aegean,
spawned Aphrodite's faultless form.
But Kronos was just as unjust
as Ouranos had been. He let
his siblings rot in Tartaros,
which made Ge mad as a hornet.

She prophesied her son would meet
the same fate as his father. What
he meted out is what he'd get.

He'd sow the seeds of his own defeat.
Kronos, to keep his offspring from
seizing the throne, used contraception.
Whenever Rhea brought forth young,
he wolfed 'em down like caramel corn.
It was sacrilegious to eat
their kids like beer nuts, Rhea thought.
The rabble might get by with that,
but it ought not go on at court.
When it came time to deliver
her next baby, Rhea vamoosed
to a secluded mountain cave whither
she secretly gave birth to Zeus.
Then, to cement the deception,
she presented Kronos a stone
in a blanket instead of her son.
He munched it like a fried wonton.
When Zeus grew up, he spiked the grog
the old souse always drank before bed
with a potent emetic. The drug
made him vomit the gods he'd ingested.
Flanked by his regurgitated
siblings and selected allies,
Zeus combated and defeated
Kronos and his corrupt cronies.

Public office attracts opposition
and Zeus no sooner took charge than
he too was the target of partisan
attack by a large, militant faction.
The giants resented the gods'
supremacy. The malicious
pinheads called for a holy jihad,
an all-out assault on Olympos.
Their sheer bulk and physical might,
their filthy locks and grimy beards,
their dragon scales instead of feet,
made them feared even by the gods.
Hurling burning oaks and boulders

at the mountaintop metropolis
like Katyusha rockets, the ogres
sparked a full-blown apocalypse.
According to ancient legend,
in order for Zeus & Co. to win,
a human had to lend a hand,
and Heracles was a shoo-in.
Transporting the hero from Cos,
where he and his crew were blown against
their wills by Hera, to Phlegra, Zeus
and his troops repelled the giants.
A general brouhaha ensued,
a theo-political convulsion.
The gods employed the weapons you'd
expect to quash the rebellion.

Zeus hurled his thunder, Poseidon
plied his trident, the Fates yelled curses,
Hephaestus slung molten iron,
Dionysus whirled his thyrsus,
Apollo drove his chariot,
Mars swung his sword, Venus cowered,
Hermes vanished in his helmet,
Hera hid and Hades glowered,
Athena practised martial arts,
Hecate sizzled them with torches,
Artemis arched, Cupid threw darts,
and Heracles slew totus porcus.

Book XV

Since all our plans eventually
fall through, why not set out to be
what we'll become intentionally:
an anecdote; comic relief?
After helping the gods demolish
the rebel giants, Heracles
set out on a quest to punish
his more egregious enemies.
It would be unconscionable
in this age of random babble
to ramble on about each battle,
so brevity will be my Bible.
At Calydon, Alcides wooed
Meleager's sister, Deianeira,
as he assured his shade he would
erewhile in Hades' eerie aura.[15]
She imbibed the love of warfare
from her father, King Oeneus.
Among those vying for her favor
was the river god Achelous.

Deianeira was overjoyed
when Heracles made his debut.
Becoming Mrs. River-God
wasn't something she aspired to.
The arrival of a rival
wasn't calculated to instill
the milk of kindness and goodwill
into Achelous' heart, but gall.
He challenged Heracles to fight.
They wrestled by the riverside.
Despite unsportsmanlike attempts to cheat,
Achelous lost both pride and bride.
The marriage began with a bang.
Both were headstrong and passionate.
Sexually they were yin and yang,
mentally more like dog and cat.

Heracles inadvertently killed
one day, during a family meal,
with a careless rap, a lad who spilled
some water from a finger bowl.
Though the death was accidental
and the boy's father forgave him,
he elected to go into exile
in accordance with Greek custom.

Thus Deianeira, overnight,
went from a palace to homeless,
forsook her former five-star life
to wander in the wilderness.
In time they came to a river,
which might have been a small matter,
but Deianeira was no swimmer
and terrified of the water.
At this juncture in the drama,
along came Nessus. The centaur
offered, for just a few drachmae,
to chauffeur the princess over.
Though Heracles wasn't a fan
of the plan, he paid his wife's fare
and waved as she and the horse-man
rode into the river together.
As they were exiting the stream,
Nessus attempted to rape her,
whereupon Heracles, hearing her scream,
reacted with tangible displeasure.
Even from that distance one could
see the centaur's body recoil
and tell the arrow's impact had
wrought injury beyond recall.

Snapping the poison arrowhead
where it protruded through his chest,
he mingled with the Hydra's blood
the seed he'd accidentally cast.
Then Nessus, in a tour de force,

convinced Deianeira his semen
could be used as a love charm in case
Heracles chased other women.
She kept a phial of the philtre
just in case, as he suggested.
When Heracles waded ashore,
the centaur was already dead.
They rented a house in Trachis
and lived happily for a while.
Deianeira gave birth to Hyllus
and they cherished their charming child.
But Heracles wasn't cut out
for a life of peace and quiet.
He was a man of action, not
some yogi on a vegan diet.
He undertook to overthrow
Oechalia's king, Eurytus, who
cheated him several years ago[16]
and was overdue for a coup.

Together with a cutthroat band
of merry mercenaries, he
slew Eurytus and his sons and
enslaved the princess Iole.
To thank the gods for his success,
he planned a lavish sacrifice
and sent Lichas, his lackey, to fetch
a brand new tunic from Trachis.
When Lichas arrived at the gate,
Deianeira quizzed the factotum,
who was only too glad to relate
everything that occurred and then some.
When he blabbed about Iole,
Deianeira became anxious
lest, led astray by her beauty,
Heracles make her his mistress.
Recalling the specious potion,
she retrieved the requested shirt
and anointed it with the poison

Nessus intended for Heracles' hurt.
Upon returning to her hall,
her heart sank, for upon the walk
smoked the potion-coated cotton ball
she'd used to daub Alcides' smock.

Heracles donned his priestly garb.
A fire crackled on the altar.
The sacrificial knives were sharp.
The lambs were ready for slaughter.
Lifting his hands to the heavens,
he lauded Zeus for his support,
as the flames heated the venom
liberally sprinkled on his shirt.
In seconds he was racked with pain
and tried to rip the tunic off,
but when he did, gobbets of skin
pulled free with every piece of cloth.
Suspecting Lichas of treason,
he seized his corporal by the feet
and flung him from the cliff whereon
they stood into the sea beneath.
Tormented thus, the son of Zeus
set sail with his crew for Trachis.
When Deianeira heard the news,
torn with remorse, she slit her wrists.
They proceeded to Mt. Oeta,
a summit where the air was pure.
Despite his wounds and raging fever,
he felled the trees to build a pyre.

When it was done he lay on top.
Reclining on his lion fleece
with his head propped against his club,
for once the hero seemed at peace.
He bid his men ignite the wood
but no one dared, afraid the deed
would haunt them ever afterward
and public scorn be their reward.

When his men refused to do it,
he asked Poeas, a shepherd who
happened by if he had a light,
in return, awarding him his bow.
As the flames rose, from overhead
fell such a freakish lightning-flash
that, when the smoke cleared it appeared
to have vaporized the pyre to ash.
Thus was fulfilled the prophecy
Dodona's priestess had foretold
that only by a dead enemy[17]
could Heracles ever be killed.

Notes

1. Mount Pholoe
2. Ten percent of the cattle
3. The sport of bull-leaping
4. She was pregnant from their first encounter.
5. The city of Abdera
6. Homer calls Paris Alexandros, meaning champion.
7. i.e. Hospitable to strangers
8. They were sons of Proteus
9. The wolf in the Reynard story cycle
10. Blind, dark, gloomy, obscure
11. See Book IV
12. The Orphic mystery cult whose rites were conducted each year at Eleusis
13. Deianeira
14. He protested the injustice of the charge by committing murder.
15. See Book XII
16. See Book XIII
17. Nessus

CPSIA information can be obtained
at www.ICGtesting.com
Printed in the USA
LVHW090012230120
644453LV00001B/52